The 30-Day Mind Reset

Transform Your Habits, Find Inner Peace, and Boost Productivity for Life

Reese Landon

Table of Contents

Introduction

Welcome to *The 30-Day Mind Reset: Transform Your Habits, Find Inner Peace, and Boost Productivity for Life*. Over the next 30 days, you'll embark on a journey of self-discovery, transformation, and growth. This isn't just a book—it's a toolkit designed to guide you through a focused period of change that will leave you feeling more aligned, energized, and in control of your life.

The Power of 30 Days
Why 30 days? Because in just a month, you can plant the seeds of lasting change. Research shows that, on average, it takes around three to four weeks to form new habits, retrain our brains, and begin to see noticeable shifts in mindset and behavior. Thirty days is short enough to commit to but long enough to yield significant results. This journey invites you to reshape your habits and renew your outlook on life in a way that feels natural and sustainable.

Whether you're hoping to boost productivity, find calm in a busy world, or simply reconnect with what truly matters to you, these 30 days are crafted to guide you every step of the way. Each week will introduce new concepts and practices, and each day offers a small, actionable step to build your momentum.

A Structured, Manageable Path to Change
This book is divided into four core areas of focus:
- **Week 1**: *Mindset and Motivation*. During this foundational week, you'll uncover what motivates you and how to replace limiting beliefs with an empowering mindset.
- **Week 2**: *Building Core Habits*. This week is all about establishing daily routines that create stability, nurture well-being, and prime you for success.
- **Week 3**: *Enhancing Productivity and Focus*. Now that your mindset is aligned and foundational habits are set, it's time to unlock new levels of focus, tackle time management, and overcome procrastination.

- **Week 4**: *Mindfulness and Inner Peace.* In the final stretch, you'll explore the tools and techniques to cultivate a peaceful, mindful life, bringing a deep sense of balance and calm to your daily experience.

These weeks are designed to build upon each other, creating a step-by-step framework for you to follow. By focusing on a specific theme each week, you'll find it easier to implement change without feeling overwhelmed or losing motivation.

The Science of Habit Formation and Transformation

Our habits are the invisible architecture of our lives. They shape our actions, influence our thoughts, and ultimately determine our reality. But habits are also malleable, which means they can be reshaped. Science shows that repeated actions—small, consistent changes—over time can rewire our brain, allowing new, healthier habits to form. This process, known as neuroplasticity, means that every time you practice a new behavior, you strengthen neural pathways in your brain, making it easier to keep that behavior in the future.

This book is based on these principles of psychology and neuroscience. Each day's activity is carefully crafted to reinforce positive habits, promote self-awareness, and gradually build a more resilient, focused, and calm mindset.

How to Use This Book

Each day in this book presents a single, focused exercise or concept that builds on what you've already accomplished. It's designed to take no more than 15–20 minutes per day. You can follow this plan at your own pace, but for the best results, try to maintain a steady rhythm without skipping too many days. If life gets in the way, don't worry; simply pick up where you left off.

For each day, bring an open mind, curiosity, and patience with yourself. Real growth happens incrementally, and every small step forward is meaningful. By showing up consistently, you're creating a habit of self-care, self-reflection, and progress that will serve you far beyond this 30-day journey.

Let this book be your companion over the next month. Embrace the challenges, celebrate your wins, and give yourself permission to explore who you are and who you're becoming. At the end of this journey, you'll find yourself more connected to your true potential, equipped with the habits and mindset to lead a fulfilling life.

Are you ready to begin? The journey to a clearer mind, a calmer heart, and a more purposeful life starts here.

Week 1: Mindset and Motivation

Day 1: Setting Intentions – What Do You Truly Want to Change?

Welcome to Day 1 of your journey. Today is about pausing to look inward and get clear on what brought you here. Change begins with intention—a focused, authentic reason that fuels everything you're working toward. Intentions go beyond surface-level desires; they are the deeper motivations that, once uncovered, give your actions power and purpose.

Why Intention Matters

An intention is like the north star of any journey. Without it, even the most structured plan can feel empty or mechanical. When you know what you truly want to change and why, you're far more likely to commit, even on the hard days. Your intention becomes your "why" for every step you take over the next 30 days.

It's normal to have a general goal like "I want to feel happier" or "I want to be more productive." But today, we'll dig a little deeper. This is about understanding what you truly want to change—not just in your day-to-day life but in how you feel, how you approach challenges, and how you relate to yourself and the world around you.

Finding Your Core Intention

To discover your true intention, ask yourself these questions and take a few minutes to write down your answers:

1. **What do I most want to improve in my life right now?**
   o Think about any habits, patterns, or feelings that may be holding you back. Do you want to change how you handle stress? Improve your focus? Let go of self-doubt?
2. **How do I want to feel by the end of these 30 days?**

o   Picture yourself a month from now. How do you feel in this vision of yourself? Calm, confident, energized, or perhaps balanced?

3. **Why is this change important to me?**
    o   Look beyond the practical benefits and explore the deeper reason. Maybe you want to feel more present with loved ones, or you're ready to move past old limitations. This is where you get specific with your "why."

4. **What impact will this change have on my life as a whole?**
    o   Think about how your life would be different if you stayed committed to this journey. Consider the ripple effect: how would it influence your relationships, your work, or your daily happiness?

Writing Your Intention Statement
Now that you've reflected on your answers, it's time to create a clear intention statement. This is a sentence or two that encapsulates what you're here to achieve and why it matters to you. Here's an example to inspire you:

- "I intend to cultivate a calm and balanced mind so that I can feel more grounded, present, and at peace with myself and others."

Or, if you're focusing on productivity:

- "I intend to build habits that boost my focus and clarity, allowing me to reach my goals with confidence and purpose."

Write your intention statement somewhere you can easily see it, perhaps in a journal or on a sticky note that you place by your bed. This will serve as a daily reminder of why you began this journey.

Daily Reflection Exercise
To end today, take a few quiet moments to sit with your intention. Close your eyes and picture yourself embodying this change. Imagine how it feels, how it impacts your day, and the kind of energy it brings to your life. Hold onto this vision; it's what you're moving toward, one day at a time.

Day 2: Identifying Limiting Beliefs and Rewriting Your Story

Today's focus is on uncovering and releasing the beliefs that hold you back. These are the silent, often subconscious, thoughts that shape how you see yourself and the world around you. We call them **limiting beliefs** because they impose invisible boundaries on what we think is possible. Whether you realize it or not, these beliefs can affect your choices, actions, and even your sense of self-worth.

By identifying these beliefs and choosing to rewrite them, you're giving yourself permission to live beyond past limitations and step into a new version of yourself.

What Are Limiting Beliefs?

Limiting beliefs are thoughts or assumptions about ourselves that restrict our growth. They often sound like "I'm not good enough," "I don't deserve success," or "I'll never change." These beliefs can stem from past experiences, cultural conditioning, or even well-meaning advice. Over time, they become so ingrained that we begin to accept them as truths, even though they're often just habits of thought.

The good news is that limiting beliefs are just that—beliefs, not facts. They can be challenged, reshaped, and ultimately transformed into empowering beliefs that serve your highest potential.

Identifying Your Limiting Beliefs

Let's start by bringing some of these beliefs into awareness. Answer the following questions to help uncover any limiting beliefs that may be influencing you:

1. **What thoughts come up when I think about my goals?**
   - Do you feel excitement, doubt, or fear? What specific thoughts pop up, especially those that seem to discourage you from taking action?
2. **What beliefs do I have about my abilities?**
   - Notice any assumptions you make about yourself. Do you tell yourself you're "not smart enough," "too shy," or "too disorganized" to achieve your goals?
3. **Where do I hold myself back the most?**

11

- o Think about areas in your life where you tend to hesitate or avoid taking risks. Are there thoughts that keep you in your comfort zone?
4. **What past experiences might have influenced these beliefs?**
   - o Reflect on past moments that shaped how you view yourself. Sometimes, even small comments or events can leave a lasting impact.

Write down any limiting beliefs that come up during this process. For example, you might notice thoughts like, "I can't start a new career at this age," or "I'm not disciplined enough to stay focused."

Rewriting Your Story
Now that you've identified some of your limiting beliefs, it's time to transform them. Take each limiting belief you wrote down and reframe it as an empowering statement. This isn't about ignoring reality; it's about choosing to see yourself through a new, more compassionate lens.

Here's how to rewrite limiting beliefs:
1. **Acknowledge the Belief**: Recognize that this belief is a story you've been telling yourself, not an unchangeable truth.
2. **Reframe the Belief**: Replace each limiting belief with a positive, empowering one that aligns with your goals. Write your new belief as if it's already true.

For example:
- Limiting Belief: "I'm too old to start over."
- New Belief: "I have the experience, wisdom, and courage to pursue my dreams at any age."
- Limiting Belief: "I'm not disciplined enough to change."
- New Belief: "I am capable of creating small, consistent habits that lead to lasting change."

3. **Visualize the New Belief**: Close your eyes and imagine yourself fully embodying this new belief. Picture yourself acting with confidence, resilience, or whatever qualities resonate with this rewritten story. See yourself moving through your day, making choices aligned with this empowering belief.

4. **Affirm and Repeat**: Each morning, remind yourself of your new beliefs. Affirmations work by creating new mental pathways, making it easier over time to think positively about yourself.

Daily Reflection Exercise

In your journal, take a moment to answer the following:

- How does it feel to let go of old, limiting beliefs?
- What changes do you notice in yourself as you embrace these new, empowering beliefs?
- What would it look like to live as though these new beliefs were true every day?

Day 3: Building a Growth Mindset for Success

Today, we're diving into the concept of the **growth mindset**—the belief that your abilities, intelligence, and potential are not fixed but can be developed through dedication and hard work. A growth mindset is more than a positive outlook; it's an approach to life that embraces challenges, persists in the face of setbacks, and sees failure as an opportunity for learning. By cultivating this mindset, you're setting yourself up for success, resilience, and continual growth.

The Power of a Growth Mindset

The growth mindset is a term popularized by psychologist Carol Dweck, who found that people with a growth mindset tend to achieve more and feel more fulfilled than those with a fixed mindset. A fixed mindset is the belief that abilities are static—that we're either "good" or "bad" at something, with no room for improvement. When we operate from a fixed mindset, we're more likely to avoid challenges, give up easily, and see effort as a sign of inadequacy.

On the other hand, a growth mindset encourages us to view challenges as a pathway to improvement, effort as a step toward mastery, and mistakes as valuable learning experiences. With this mindset, you become more adaptable, more resilient, and more open to change—all essential qualities for reaching your goals.

Shifting from Fixed to Growth

Let's explore a few common fixed mindset thoughts and see how we can reframe them into growth-oriented beliefs:

1. **Fixed Mindset**: "I'm just not good at this."
    - **Growth Mindset**: "I can learn to get better with practice and time."
2. **Fixed Mindset**: "If I don't succeed right away, it means I'll never succeed."
    - **Growth Mindset**: "Every setback is a step toward learning what I need to improve. I'll get better with each attempt."
3. **Fixed Mindset**: "I don't have the talent for this."

14

- ○ **Growth Mindset**: "With effort, patience, and practice, I can develop this skill over time."

As you notice your own thoughts throughout the day, look out for fixed mindset language and reframe it. With practice, you'll start to see obstacles as opportunities, and you'll develop greater confidence in your ability to grow.

Building Your Growth Mindset Muscle

Developing a growth mindset takes time and consistent effort, much like building a muscle. Here are some practical steps to help you strengthen your growth mindset each day:

1. **Embrace Challenges**: Seek out challenges that push you beyond your comfort zone. Whether it's a new skill, a tough project, or an unfamiliar activity, approach each challenge with curiosity. Remember, the goal isn't to succeed immediately but to learn and grow through the experience.

2. **Celebrate Effort Over Outcome**: Rather than focusing solely on results, recognize and celebrate the effort you put in. This shifts your attention from "I succeeded" or "I failed" to "I made progress." Effort is a crucial part of growth, and acknowledging it reinforces the value of persistence.

3. **Reframe Failures as Learning Experiences**: Every time you stumble or face a setback, ask yourself, "What can I learn from this?" This simple question shifts your focus from frustration to growth. Mistakes are often the best teachers, and with a growth mindset, you'll find that each failure brings you closer to improvement.

4. **Practice Self-Compassion**: Building a growth mindset doesn't mean you have to be hard on yourself. Self-compassion allows you to be kind and patient with yourself, especially when you're struggling. Embrace the fact that growth is a journey, not a destination.

5. **Set Small, Achievable Goals**: Choose goals that challenge you but feel manageable. Each time you achieve one, no matter how small, you reinforce your belief in your capacity to learn and grow.

Daily Reflection Exercise

Today, take a few minutes to reflect on a time when you faced a challenge or setback. Answer these questions in your journal:

- What was the challenge, and how did you initially react?
- If you were to approach this challenge with a growth mindset, how would your perspective or actions change?
- What lessons did you (or could you) learn from this experience?

Growth Mindset Affirmations

To help reinforce your growth mindset, try using affirmations. Here are a few to get started:

- "I am constantly learning and growing."
- "Challenges are opportunities for growth."
- "My effort and dedication will lead to improvement."

Repeat these affirmations each morning or whenever you need a reminder of your potential.

Day 4: The Power of Positive Affirmations – Speaking Change Into Existence

Today, we're exploring the transformative practice of **positive affirmations**. Affirmations are short, powerful statements that you repeat to yourself, consciously focusing on the qualities, mindset, or outcomes you want to cultivate. This practice is rooted in the idea that our thoughts shape our reality—when we consistently feed our minds with positive, empowering beliefs, we start to see changes in how we think, feel, and act.

Affirmations are not just feel-good statements; they're a tool for rewiring your brain. When used consistently, they can help dismantle negative thought patterns and replace them with positive, constructive beliefs that align with the person you're becoming.

Why Affirmations Work

Affirmations work on a neurological level. When you repeat an affirmation, you activate your brain's reward centers, creating new pathways in the brain. Over time, these neural pathways become stronger, making it easier for your mind to default to positive thoughts rather than negative ones. This is called **neuroplasticity**, or the brain's ability to reorganize itself by forming new neural connections.

In short, affirmations help shift your self-perception. By consistently speaking positive statements about who you are and what you're capable of, you build the foundation for a mindset that believes in growth, resilience, and possibility.

Crafting Your Personal Affirmations

To get the most out of affirmations, make them specific, positive, and aligned with the changes you want to see. Follow these guidelines to create powerful affirmations:

1. **Start with "I am"**: This phrase grounds the affirmation in your identity, affirming that it's part of who you are. Example: "I am confident and capable of achieving my goals."

2. **Keep it in the present tense**: Use language that reflects that you already embody this quality. Instead of saying "I will be successful," say "I am successful."
3. **Be specific and positive**: Avoid vague or negative phrasing. Rather than saying "I am not anxious," try "I am calm and at peace in every situation."
4. **Align with your values and goals**: Ensure that each affirmation is meaningful to you. Think about the qualities you want to cultivate and the obstacles you're overcoming.

Here are a few example affirmations to inspire you:

- "I am resilient, confident, and able to handle whatever comes my way."
- "I am worthy of love, happiness, and success."
- "I am focused, productive, and moving closer to my goals every day."
- "I attract positivity, gratitude, and growth into my life."

How to Use Affirmations

For affirmations to be effective, consistency is key. Incorporate them into your daily routine to make them a natural part of your life. Here are some tips for using affirmations daily:

1. **Repeat Them Each Morning**: Start your day with 5-10 minutes dedicated to saying or writing your affirmations. This primes your mind for a positive outlook all day.
2. **Say Them Out Loud**: Speaking affirmations out loud, with intention and emotion, strengthens their impact. Stand in front of a mirror, make eye contact with yourself, and say each affirmation as if you already believe it.
3. **Write Them Down**: Keeping a journal of your affirmations helps you internalize them. You could also keep them on sticky notes around your home, workspace, or in your phone for reminders throughout the day.
4. **Visualize**: As you repeat each affirmation, close your eyes and imagine yourself embodying that quality. Visualize what it feels like, what your day would look like, and how you would carry yourself.

5. **Use Affirmations During Challenging Moments**: When self-doubt or negative thoughts arise, combat them with your affirmations. This practice reinforces your new, empowering beliefs and diminishes old, limiting patterns.

Daily Reflection Exercise

In your journal, reflect on the following questions to deepen your connection with your affirmations:

- Which affirmations resonate with me most and why?
- How do I feel when I repeat my affirmations? Do I feel empowered, calm, inspired?
- What changes do I notice in my thoughts and emotions as I practice daily affirmations?

Sample Affirmation Routine

1. **Morning**: Repeat 3-5 affirmations that align with your daily intentions. Speak them with conviction, and feel the energy of each word as you say it.
2. **Afternoon**: Take a moment to reflect on your affirmations or write them down. Remind yourself of your focus and goals.
3. **Evening**: Before bed, repeat your affirmations again, imagining the person you are becoming. Visualize these positive beliefs as you drift off to sleep.

Day 5: Practicing Self-Compassion – Embracing Imperfection

Today's focus is on something that can be transformative yet often overlooked: **self-compassion**. In a world that frequently pushes us toward perfection and constant improvement, self-compassion is the reminder that we are worthy of kindness, even in our struggles. It's the practice of meeting ourselves with understanding and patience rather than criticism, especially when things don't go as planned. Self-compassion isn't about letting ourselves off the hook—it's about embracing our imperfections as part of our humanity and treating ourselves with the same kindness we'd offer a friend.

Why Self-Compassion Matters

Many of us are quick to show kindness to others, but when it comes to ourselves, we can be our own harshest critics. Self-compassion is about shifting that inner voice from judgmental to nurturing. Research by Dr. Kristin Neff, a pioneer in self-compassion studies, shows that people who practice self-compassion tend to be more resilient, motivated, and happier. This is because self-compassion provides a safe space to acknowledge mistakes, learn from them, and move forward without getting stuck in a cycle of self-criticism.

Self-compassion has three main components:

1. **Self-Kindness**: Being gentle and understanding with yourself, rather than harshly critical.
2. **Common Humanity**: Recognizing that everyone makes mistakes and experiences pain; you're not alone in your struggles.
3. **Mindfulness**: Acknowledging your emotions without letting them overwhelm you or define you.

Embracing Imperfection

Perfectionism is often rooted in the belief that our worth is tied to our achievements or that we must meet impossible standards to be "enough." But embracing imperfection allows us to grow, make mistakes, and live more freely. Today, we'll work on loosening the grip of perfectionism and opening ourselves up to a mindset that values progress over perfection.

Steps to Practice Self-Compassion

Here's how you can start cultivating self-compassion and embracing your imperfections:

1. **Notice Your Inner Critic**: Pay attention to how you speak to yourself, especially in moments of difficulty or frustration. Are your words harsh, judgmental, or unkind? Awareness is the first step to change.
2. **Shift to Self-Kindness**: When you catch yourself being critical, pause and consider how you would speak to a friend in the same situation. Replace judgmental thoughts with gentle, understanding ones. Instead of "I always mess things up," try, "I'm doing the best I can, and it's okay to make mistakes."
3. **Practice Common Humanity**: Remind yourself that everyone struggles and makes mistakes. This can be as simple as saying, "I'm not alone in this," or "Other people feel this way too." Acknowledging your shared humanity makes it easier to let go of feelings of inadequacy.
4. **Stay Mindful of Your Emotions**: Notice what you're feeling without judging it. Allow yourself to feel disappointment, frustration, or sadness without immediately trying to "fix" it. Emotions are temporary, and by simply observing them, you give yourself space to process without self-blame.
5. **Affirm Your Worth**: Self-compassion isn't about boosting your ego; it's about recognizing that you have worth simply because you exist. Remind yourself that your value isn't tied to perfection. Repeat affirmations like, "I am worthy as I am," or "I accept myself fully, flaws and all."

Daily Reflection Exercise

Take a few moments to answer these questions in your journal:
- **What would it look like to treat myself with kindness today?**
- **What's one area of my life where I tend to be overly critical? How could I approach it with more compassion?**
- **How does it feel to let go of the need for perfection, even if just for today?**

Self-Compassion Meditation
Try this short, guided meditation to deepen your self-compassion:
1. **Find a comfortable, quiet space** where you can sit or lie down without distractions.
2. **Close your eyes** and take a few deep breaths, letting go of any tension as you exhale.
3. **Place a hand over your heart**, and take a moment to feel its warmth. Imagine this hand is a symbol of kindness, a reminder to treat yourself gently.
4. **Silently repeat a few phrases** to yourself, such as:
   o "May I be kind to myself."
   o "May I accept myself as I am."
   o "May I give myself the compassion I need."
5. Allow any feelings of comfort, peace, or acceptance to fill you, even if only for a few moments.

Practicing Self-Compassion Throughout the Day
Self-compassion isn't something you need to reserve for specific moments. Practice it throughout the day by:
- Taking deep breaths when you feel stressed, reminding yourself, "It's okay. I'm doing my best."
- Giving yourself permission to take breaks without guilt.
- Being patient with yourself when things don't go as planned or when you face challenges.

Day 6: Visualization Techniques for Motivation

Today's focus is on the power of **visualization**—a practice that leverages the mind's ability to create vivid, mental images of desired outcomes, fueling motivation and shaping our actions. Visualization isn't just daydreaming; it's an intentional and active process that helps you mentally rehearse success, preparing your mind and body for real-life achievement. Athletes, business leaders, and creatives alike use visualization to enhance performance, boost confidence, and stay motivated on their journeys.

When you visualize a goal, you engage the same neural networks in your brain that would activate if you were physically doing the activity. This means that your brain can be "trained" for success by simply imagining it in detail. Visualization helps you clarify your goals, foster belief in your abilities, and ignite the motivation to take action.

How Visualization Works

Visualization connects our mind and body, making it a powerful tool for change. By vividly imagining yourself achieving your goals, you strengthen your commitment to them. Studies show that when we visualize success, we activate the brain's reward system, releasing dopamine—a neurotransmitter associated with motivation and pleasure. This helps us associate positive emotions with our goals, making it easier to stay motivated even when challenges arise.

Visualization has two main types:

1. **Outcome Visualization**: Focusing on the result you want to achieve.
2. **Process Visualization**: Focusing on the steps you'll take to reach your goal.

Both forms are valuable, but combining them creates a powerful visualization practice that builds motivation and momentum.

Steps for Effective Visualization

Here's a step-by-step guide to create a daily visualization practice that fuels your motivation:

1. **Set Aside Quiet Time**: Find a comfortable, quiet space where you can be alone for a few minutes without distractions. Relax your mind and body, taking a few deep breaths.
2. **Clarify Your Goal**: Identify a specific goal you want to achieve, something meaningful and motivating. Visualize this goal as clearly as possible, imagining it in detail.
3. **Engage All Your Senses**: The more vivid your visualization, the more effective it will be. Imagine what achieving your goal looks like, feels like, even smells and sounds like. Engage your senses to make the vision feel as real as possible.
4. **Visualize the Outcome**: Picture yourself having already achieved your goal. Imagine how it feels to reach it, the pride, joy, or sense of accomplishment. Embrace the positive emotions that arise and let them fill you with motivation.
5. **Visualize the Process**: Now, shift your focus to the steps you need to take to reach your goal. Imagine yourself moving through each step confidently, overcoming any obstacles with ease. This part of visualization helps prepare you mentally for the actual work and keeps you motivated to stay on track.
6. **Anchor the Feeling**: Before ending your visualization, focus on the positive emotions you've generated. Take a moment to "anchor" these feelings by breathing deeply and feeling them throughout your body. Anchoring reinforces the connection between the vision and your motivation.

Daily Visualization Routine
To make visualization a consistent practice, try incorporating it into your morning or evening routine. Spend just 5–10 minutes each day visualizing your goals with the steps above. This regular practice strengthens your motivation and helps you stay connected to your "why."

Visualization Prompts for Motivation
Here are some prompts to guide your visualization session:
- **How does achieving this goal positively impact my life?**
- **What steps am I confidently taking each day to reach this goal?**

- **How do I feel once I've reached my goal? What emotions arise?**

Answering these questions mentally while you visualize will create a clearer, stronger mental image of success.

Overcoming Common Visualization Challenges

If you find it challenging to visualize, don't worry—like any skill, it gets easier with practice. Here are some tips to help:
- **Use Physical Reminders**: If visualizing feels difficult, try looking at pictures, quotes, or objects that represent your goal before you start. These can serve as mental cues to enhance your visualization.
- **Write it Down First**: If you're struggling to imagine your goal clearly, write a description of it. Then, use this written image as a mental blueprint for your visualization.
- **Stay Patient**: Visualization is a skill that improves over time. If it feels unclear at first, stick with it—your mind will gradually become better at forming detailed mental images.

Daily Reflection Exercise

After your visualization session, take a moment to reflect in your journal:
- How did it feel to visualize my goal and the steps to reach it?
- What emotions did I experience as I imagined myself succeeding?
- How does this visualization impact my motivation moving forward?

Visualization Affirmations

To strengthen your motivation, try pairing your visualization practice with affirmations that support your goals:
- "I see my goals clearly, and I am motivated to bring them to life."
- "Every step I take brings me closer to my vision of success."
- "I am capable, prepared, and ready to achieve my dreams."

Day 7: Reflecting on Week 1 – Celebrating Small Wins

Congratulations on completing your first week of the 30-Day Mind Reset journey! Today is dedicated to reflection and celebration. Over the past six days, you've taken powerful steps toward a more purposeful mindset, exploring intentions, beliefs, and techniques that support your growth. Acknowledge that each step, no matter how small, has laid a foundation for positive change.

Why Celebrating Small Wins Matters

Celebrating small wins is an essential part of personal growth. It's easy to overlook small achievements in favor of big goals, but research shows that recognizing small progress releases dopamine, the "feel-good" neurotransmitter. This boost in motivation reinforces the behavior, making it more likely that you'll stay on track. By pausing to celebrate, you're training your mind to focus on progress rather than perfection, building confidence and maintaining motivation as you move forward.

Reflecting on Your Week

Take a few minutes to reflect on the journey so far. These reflections will help solidify your efforts, increase self-awareness, and highlight the shifts you've begun to make.

Reflection Prompts

1. **What intentions did I set at the start of this week, and how do I feel about them now?**
   - Reflect on the intentions you set on Day 1. Do they still feel aligned with your goals? Have they evolved in any way?
2. **What new insights have I gained about myself?**
   - Consider the discoveries you made about your beliefs, mindset, and personal strengths. What surprised you? What resonates most?
3. **What small wins have I achieved this week?**

26

o These could be anything from completing a daily exercise to catching yourself in self-critical moments and choosing self-compassion instead. Acknowledge each win, no matter how small.

4. **How have I noticed my mindset shifting?**
    o Have you become more aware of limiting beliefs? Are you starting to reframe challenges more positively? Celebrate any changes, even if they feel subtle.

5. **What am I grateful for in this process?**
    o Gratitude deepens your experience by connecting you with the positive aspects of this journey. What has made you feel grateful this week?

Celebrating Your Progress

Take a moment to celebrate the effort and growth you've put in this week. Celebrating doesn't have to be grand; it's about recognizing yourself for the commitment you've shown. Here are a few simple ways to honor your progress:

- **Write a Note of Appreciation to Yourself**: In your journal, write a short note thanking yourself for showing up each day. Recognize the courage it takes to create change and let yourself feel proud.
- **Share Your Wins with a Friend or Loved One**: Talking about your small victories can amplify their impact. Share something positive from this week with someone supportive, even if it's just a small observation.
- **Treat Yourself**: Reward yourself with a little something that makes you feel good—a favorite snack, a relaxing bath, or a peaceful moment outside. Treating yourself reinforces that you're deserving of recognition and care.

Setting Intentions for the Next Week

As you move into Week 2, consider what you'd like to carry forward from this week and what you're excited to build upon. Setting a simple intention for the coming week can help you stay focused and motivated.

- **What quality or mindset do I want to strengthen next week?** (e.g., "I want to continue practicing self-compassion," or "I want to stay open to growth and change.")
- **What small daily action can I commit to?** (e.g., "I'll remind myself of my intentions each morning" or "I'll journal my thoughts each evening.")

Daily Reflection Exercise
In your journal, answer the following prompts to capture your reflections and celebration:
- What am I most proud of from this week?
- How do I feel about the progress I've made so far?
- What's one thing I want to remember as I move into next week?

Week 2: Building Core Habits for Success

Day 8: Morning Rituals to Set the Tone for Your Day

Welcome to Week 2, where we focus on building core habits that create stability, nurture well-being, and lay the groundwork for a fulfilling day. Today's focus is on creating a **morning ritual**—a consistent, intentional way to start your day that sets a positive, purposeful tone.

A morning ritual isn't just a series of tasks; it's a commitment to beginning each day with clarity, intention, and calm. When you dedicate the first moments of your day to self-care and grounding practices, you're signaling to yourself that your well-being and goals matter. A well-designed morning ritual can improve focus, boost mood, and help you approach the day with a mindset primed for productivity and positivity.

Why Morning Rituals Matter

Your first actions and thoughts in the morning often set the course for the rest of the day. If you start your day with calm, mindful practices, you're more likely to stay centered and intentional even when challenges arise. A morning ritual provides a stable anchor, helping you begin the day with clarity rather than rushing or reacting to stress.

Many successful people use morning rituals to fuel their creativity, focus, and resilience. When you cultivate your own, you're giving yourself a foundation that supports your growth and helps you move through the day with purpose.

Building Your Morning Ritual

A morning ritual doesn't have to be complicated or time-consuming. Start with 15–30 minutes and choose practices that resonate with you. Over time, you can adjust and refine your routine based on what feels most nourishing. Here's a step-by-step guide to help you create a morning ritual that aligns with your needs:

1. **Begin with Stillness (5 Minutes)**:
   - Take a few moments to sit quietly upon waking. Focus on your breathing, letting each inhale and exhale relax you. This brief period of stillness grounds you before diving into the day and gives your mind space to ease into wakefulness.
   - Alternatively, you could try a quick, guided meditation or simply practice mindful breathing for a few minutes.

2. **Set an Intention for the Day (2 Minutes)**:
   - Reflect on what you want from the day. Choose a simple intention such as "Today, I will approach challenges with calm" or "I intend to find moments of joy in my day."
   - Setting an intention gives your day a sense of purpose and helps guide your decisions and reactions.

3. **Practice Gratitude (2 Minutes)**:
   - Take a moment to think of three things you're grateful for. These can be small, like the comfort of your bed, or big, like a supportive friend or family member.
   - Gratitude shifts your focus to the positive, fostering an open, appreciative mindset.

4. **Move Your Body (5–10 Minutes)**:
   - Gentle movement, whether through stretching, yoga, or a brisk walk, wakes up your body and boosts energy. Movement releases endorphins, helping you feel more alert and positive.
   - You don't need an intense workout; just a few mindful stretches can make a big difference in your energy and mood.

5. **Visualize Your Day (2–5 Minutes)**:
   - Take a few minutes to visualize how you want your day to unfold. Picture yourself moving through your tasks with focus, handling challenges with calm, and ending the day feeling accomplished.

o   Visualization is a powerful tool for motivation and helps prime your mind for success.
6. **Fuel Your Body**:
   o   Before diving into your responsibilities, nourish yourself with a healthy breakfast or a glass of water with lemon. Providing your body with essential nutrients in the morning supports your energy and concentration throughout the day.

Sample Morning Ritual

Here's a sample routine based on the steps above:
1. **Sit Quietly and Breathe** – 5 minutes
2. **Set an Intention** – 2 minutes
3. **Gratitude Practice** – 2 minutes
4. **Gentle Stretching** – 5 minutes
5. **Visualize Your Day** – 2 minutes
6. **Nourish Yourself** – Enjoy a glass of water or a simple breakfast

Tips for Making Your Morning Ritual Stick
1. **Start Small**: Choose just two or three elements from the list above if a full ritual feels overwhelming. You can gradually build your routine as it becomes a habit.
2. **Consistency Over Perfection**: Aim to practice your ritual consistently, even if some days are shorter than others. Consistency is more important than length.
3. **Customize It**: Feel free to adjust each element to fit your needs. Your morning ritual should feel personal and meaningful to you.

Reflection Exercise

In your journal, reflect on the following questions:
- **How does my current morning routine make me feel?**
- **What changes could I make to bring more calm and intention to my mornings?**
- **How does it feel to dedicate time to myself at the start of each day?**

Evening Prep for a Smoother Morning

One way to set yourself up for a successful morning is to prepare the night before. Take a few minutes each evening to organize your space, lay out clothes, or write down a quick to-do list. This minimizes morning decisions, helping you focus on your ritual without distractions.

Day 9: Designing an Evening Routine for Rest and Reflection

Today, we're focusing on creating a calming **evening routine** that helps you unwind, reflect, and set yourself up for restful sleep. Just as a morning routine sets a positive tone for your day, an evening routine allows you to release the day's stresses, bring closure to any lingering thoughts, and transition into a state of relaxation. By intentionally winding down, you're more likely to get quality rest, which in turn improves your focus, mood, and resilience for the day ahead.

An evening routine isn't about accomplishing more tasks; it's a gentle ritual to ease into the night, bringing your day to a peaceful close and preparing your mind and body for the rest they need.

Why an Evening Routine Matters

Our days are often filled with stimulation, from screens and social interactions to problem-solving and task management. Without a clear transition to rest, it's common for our minds to stay active, making it harder to relax and fall asleep. A well-crafted evening routine helps signal to your brain that it's time to slow down. When practiced consistently, it can improve the quality of your sleep, reduce stress, and help you wake up feeling refreshed and ready for the day.

Creating Your Evening Routine

Your evening routine doesn't need to be elaborate or lengthy. It's about choosing a few calming practices that help you reflect, release tension, and prepare for restorative sleep. Here's a guide to creating a simple, effective evening routine:

1. **Set a Consistent Bedtime**:

o Choose a time for bed that allows you to get adequate sleep, ideally 7–9 hours. Going to bed and waking up at the same time each day helps regulate your body's internal clock, making it easier to fall asleep and wake up naturally.

2. **Turn Off Screens (30–60 Minutes Before Bed)**:
   o The blue light from phones, tablets, and computers can interfere with your body's production of melatonin, a hormone that regulates sleep. Try to avoid screens at least 30 minutes before bed to support your body's natural sleep cycle.

3. **Reflect on the Day (5–10 Minutes)**:
   o Take a few moments to reflect on your day. You can do this through journaling, mentally reviewing your day, or expressing gratitude. Reflecting helps bring closure to the day, allowing you to leave behind any stress or unresolved thoughts.

4. **Practice Gratitude**:
   o Reflect on three things you're grateful for from the day, big or small. Gratitude shifts your focus to positive experiences, fostering a sense of contentment and peace.

5. **Prepare for Tomorrow (5–10 Minutes)**:
   o Write down any tasks or thoughts for the next day, clearing your mind of anything that might keep you up. You might also set out clothes or prepare items you'll need in the morning. This small act of preparation reduces decision-making in the morning and helps you feel organized and ready.

6. **Engage in a Relaxing Activity**:
   o Choose an activity that relaxes you and helps you unwind. This could be reading a book, listening to calming music, gentle stretching, or practicing deep breathing. Avoid stimulating activities like intense exercise or work-related tasks.

7. **Practice Deep Breathing or Meditation (5 Minutes)**:

- Take a few minutes for mindful breathing or meditation. This practice calms the mind, reduces stress, and signals to your body that it's time to rest. You might try a simple breathing technique, like inhaling for four counts, holding for four, and exhaling for four.

8. **Dim the Lights**:
   - Reduce the lighting in your room as bedtime approaches. Lower lighting signals to your brain that it's time to wind down, supporting the release of melatonin.

Sample Evening Routine

Here's an example of a calming evening routine based on the steps above:

1. **Turn Off Screens** – 30 minutes before bed
2. **Reflect on the Day & Practice Gratitude** – 5 minutes
3. **Prepare for Tomorrow** – 5 minutes
4. **Relaxing Activity** – 10–15 minutes (reading, listening to calming music)
5. **Deep Breathing Exercise** – 5 minutes
6. **Dim Lights and Prepare for Bed**

Tips for Sticking to Your Evening Routine

1. **Start Small**: If a full routine feels overwhelming, start with just one or two calming activities and gradually add more as you feel ready.
2. **Consistency Over Perfection**: Aim to follow your routine consistently, but be flexible when needed. Missing a day isn't a setback; simply resume the next night.
3. **Customize for Comfort**: Your evening routine should feel nourishing and enjoyable. Adjust the activities or timing to suit your personal preferences and lifestyle.

Evening Reflection Exercise

In your journal, reflect on the following:

- **What activities help me feel calm and relaxed at night?**
- **Are there any current habits in my evening routine that keep me alert or stressed? How could I replace them?**

- **What small change could I make tonight to improve my rest?**

Preparing Your Mind for Tomorrow

As part of your evening routine, consider ending with a simple intention for the next day. For example, "Tomorrow, I'll approach my tasks with focus and calm," or "I will be gentle with myself as I work toward my goals." Setting an intention prepares your mind for a positive start to the morning, creating a sense of continuity in your growth journey.

Day 10: Establishing a Journaling Habit for Mental Clarity

Today's focus is on developing a **journaling habit** to promote mental clarity, self-awareness, and emotional balance. Journaling is a simple but powerful tool that allows you to process thoughts, explore emotions, and reflect on your growth. It's like having a conversation with yourself—a space to release what's on your mind, clarify your goals, and document your journey.

Establishing a regular journaling practice can help you make sense of complex feelings, reduce stress, and uncover insights that might otherwise go unnoticed. When you write, you create a private, judgment-free zone where you can be completely honest, which often leads to greater self-understanding and clarity.

The Benefits of Journaling for Mental Clarity

Journaling has a unique way of bringing order to inner chaos. When you take your thoughts from your mind and put them on paper, they become easier to manage and understand. Studies have shown that journaling can reduce anxiety, boost creativity, and improve problem-solving skills. Journaling also helps us notice patterns in our thoughts and emotions, making it easier to understand what influences our moods and actions.

By developing this habit, you're cultivating a practice of reflection that helps you focus, let go of stress, and approach each day with greater clarity and calm.

Getting Started with Journaling

If you're new to journaling or unsure where to begin, don't worry—there's no "right" way to do it. The key is consistency and openness. Here's a step-by-step guide to help you establish a journaling habit:

1. **Choose a Dedicated Time and Place**:
   o Decide on a time that works best for you, whether it's morning, evening, or even a midday break. Settle into a quiet space where you won't be interrupted, and make journaling a mindful ritual rather than a rushed task.
2. **Begin with a Few Minutes**:

- o If journaling feels overwhelming, start small. Dedicate just 5–10 minutes each day to writing. Over time, you may find yourself naturally wanting to write more, but starting with a few minutes helps ease you into the habit.
3. **Write Freely, Without Judgment**:
   - o Allow yourself to write whatever comes to mind without worrying about grammar, spelling, or structure. This is your private space, and there's no need to censor or edit yourself. Trust that whatever flows from your pen is worth exploring.
4. **Use Prompts if Needed**:
   - o If you're not sure what to write, use prompts to guide your thoughts. Prompts can help you focus on specific areas, like your goals, emotions, or recent experiences. (See some example prompts below to get started.)
5. **Reflect on Your Day and Your Feelings**:
   - o Spend a few minutes each day reflecting on what happened, how it made you feel, and any insights or observations. Journaling about your day-to-day life can help you understand yourself better and identify what supports or detracts from your well-being.

Journaling Prompts for Mental Clarity

Here are some prompts to help you dive deeper and bring clarity to your thoughts:

1. **What is currently on my mind, and how does it make me feel?**
2. **What are my top three priorities today, and why do they matter to me?**
3. **What challenges am I facing, and how could I approach them with a fresh perspective?**
4. **What am I grateful for today?**
5. **What is one thing I've learned recently that has impacted me?**
6. **How would I like to feel by the end of this week, and what steps could help me get there?**

You can choose a single prompt each day or explore different ones depending on your needs and mood. Allow these prompts to serve as starting points; feel free to expand beyond them if other thoughts come up.

Tips for Making Journaling a Consistent Habit

1. **Make it Enjoyable**: Use a notebook that you enjoy writing in, or light a candle to create a calming atmosphere. Treat journaling as a relaxing ritual rather than a chore.

2. **Don't Overthink It**: Your journal is a safe space, and there's no need for perfection. Write what feels right, and let go of the need to "do it correctly."

3. **Reflect on Progress**: Once a week or at the end of each month, look back on your entries. Reflecting on past thoughts can reveal growth, identify patterns, and remind you of your journey.

Daily Reflection Exercise

In your journal, take a few moments to answer the following questions to establish a sense of purpose with your journaling:

- **How do I feel after journaling today?**
- **Did I uncover any new insights or emotions during today's session?**
- **What would I like to explore further in my journal tomorrow?**

Using Journaling for Stress Relief

If you feel overwhelmed, journaling can also serve as a release for stress and negative emotions. Try a "brain dump" where you let all your thoughts flow onto the page without structure or purpose. This can help clear your mind and bring a sense of relief, especially on stressful days.

Another technique is **gratitude journaling**: write down three things you're grateful for each day. Studies show that gratitude journaling can improve mental health, promote optimism, and increase feelings of joy.

Day 11: Practicing Daily Gratitude – Shifting Your Focus

Today's focus is on **gratitude**—a simple yet transformative practice that helps us shift our attention from what might be lacking to what we already have. Gratitude is more than a fleeting emotion; it's a perspective that brings our minds back to moments of appreciation, fostering a sense of contentment and joy. By integrating gratitude into your daily routine, you cultivate a mindset that recognizes abundance rather than scarcity, and this shift can profoundly impact your outlook, resilience, and overall well-being.

Gratitude doesn't ignore life's challenges, but it helps balance them by drawing attention to the positive. When we regularly practice gratitude, we train our brains to see goodness even in small things, creating a more optimistic and fulfilled mindset.

The Power of Daily Gratitude

Studies show that people who practice gratitude regularly experience less stress, greater happiness, and improved mental health. Gratitude activates the brain's reward system, releasing dopamine and serotonin—neurotransmitters associated with happiness and relaxation. Over time, a daily gratitude practice rewires your brain to notice and appreciate positives more easily, helping you build a sense of inner peace and resilience.

Getting Started with Your Gratitude Practice

Gratitude is most effective when practiced consistently, and it doesn't require much time. Just a few minutes each day can make a meaningful difference. Here's how to begin:

1. **Set Aside a Moment Each Day**: Choose a consistent time for gratitude practice, such as in the morning to start your day positively, or in the evening to reflect on the day's blessings. Dedicate just 5–10 minutes to this practice.
2. **Write Down Three Things You're Grateful For**:
   - In your journal, list three things you're grateful for each day. These can be big or small, such as a meaningful conversation, a warm cup of tea, or simply a moment of quiet.

- Writing down your gratitude helps reinforce it in your mind, making the practice more intentional and memorable.

3. **Be Specific and Personal**:
   - The more specific you are with your gratitude, the more meaningful it becomes. Instead of writing "I'm grateful for my family," try "I'm grateful for my sister's encouraging words today."
   - Focusing on details deepens your appreciation, helping you connect emotionally to the things you're grateful for.

4. **Reflect on Why You're Grateful**:
   - After listing each item, take a moment to reflect on why it matters to you. For example, if you're grateful for a supportive friend, think about how their support positively impacts your life. This step enhances the emotional benefit of gratitude, strengthening the connection to your feelings of appreciation.

Expanding Your Gratitude Practice

To deepen your gratitude practice, try some of these additional exercises:

- **Gratitude Meditation**: Spend a few minutes in quiet reflection, thinking about the things you're grateful for. Visualize each one in detail, allowing a feeling of warmth and appreciation to grow.
- **Gratitude Letters**: Write a short letter to someone you appreciate, expressing your gratitude. You don't necessarily need to send it; simply writing it can help you feel more connected and appreciative.
- **Gratitude Jar**: Keep a small jar and add a note each day with something you're grateful for. At the end of the month or year, read through these notes to remind yourself of the blessings you've experienced.

Practicing Gratitude in Difficult Times

It's natural to feel grateful when life is going well, but gratitude is even more powerful when practiced during challenging times. On hard days, shift your focus to small, grounding things you might normally overlook. Maybe it's the feeling of a cozy blanket, the support of a loved one, or even the resilience you're showing in facing your challenges. This practice helps you find light even when things feel dark, fostering a sense of strength and perspective.

Reflection Exercise

In your journal, answer these questions to explore the impact of gratitude on your day-to-day life:

- **How do I feel after practicing gratitude today?**
- **What difference do I notice in my mood or outlook after listing things I'm grateful for?**
- **How can I integrate gratitude more deeply into my daily life?**

Gratitude Affirmations

Affirmations can help reinforce a grateful mindset. Here are a few to inspire you:

- "I am grateful for all that I have and all that I am becoming."
- "Today, I choose to focus on the good and appreciate the blessings in my life."
- "Every day brings new opportunities for gratitude and growth."

A Simple Daily Gratitude Routine

1. **Morning**: As you wake up, take a moment to think of one thing you're grateful for that morning. It could be as simple as the chance to start a new day.
2. **Throughout the Day**: When you encounter something positive, pause briefly to acknowledge it with a sense of gratitude. This could be as small as a kind gesture or a beautiful moment in nature.
3. **Evening**: In your journal, write down three things you're grateful for that day. Reflect on each one and allow yourself to feel the appreciation fully.

Day 11: Practicing Daily Gratitude – Shifting Your Focus

Today's focus is on **gratitude**—a practice that gently guides our minds from what's lacking to what's abundant in our lives. Gratitude is more than a pleasant feeling; it's a choice to notice and appreciate the positives, both big and small. When we practice gratitude daily, we shift our focus toward what's going well, nurturing a mindset that celebrates life's moments and fosters resilience, even during challenges.

Gratitude has the power to transform how we experience the world. Rather than waiting for things to improve or become "perfect," gratitude teaches us to find joy in the present and recognize blessings in the here and now. Over time, this habit creates a foundation of contentment, helping us feel more connected to ourselves, our loved ones, and our surroundings.

Why Daily Gratitude Matters

When practiced regularly, gratitude can change the way our brains perceive the world. Studies show that gratitude stimulates the brain's reward system, releasing dopamine and serotonin—neurotransmitters that boost our mood and increase feelings of happiness and calm. Practicing gratitude regularly helps us build a habit of positivity, making it easier to see the good around us, even on difficult days.

Gratitude can be transformative because it's an act of perspective. It allows us to pause, appreciate, and fully experience what's often overlooked, helping us find meaning and value in our day-to-day lives.

Getting Started with Your Gratitude Practice

Building a daily gratitude practice is simple but profound. You only need a few minutes each day to start noticing and appreciating life's gifts. Here's a step-by-step guide to help you incorporate gratitude into your routine:

1. **Set a Dedicated Time**:

o Decide on a specific time each day to practice gratitude, such as in the morning when you wake up, or in the evening before bed. A consistent time helps make it a habit, ensuring that gratitude becomes a regular part of your day.

2. **Write Down Three Things You're Grateful For**:
   o In a journal or notebook, list three things you're grateful for each day. These don't have to be grand; small, simple moments count just as much. It could be the warmth of your coffee, a conversation with a friend, or a moment of quiet.
   o Writing your thoughts down makes your gratitude practice intentional and reinforces the habit.

3. **Be Specific and Personal**:
   o Focusing on specifics can deepen your experience of gratitude. For example, instead of writing "I'm grateful for my family," try "I'm grateful for my sister's encouragement today."
   o When you highlight the details, your gratitude feels more meaningful and genuine, connecting you to the unique blessings in your life.

4. **Reflect on Why You're Grateful**:
   o As you list each item, take a moment to consider why it's meaningful to you. Reflecting on the "why" helps you experience gratitude more fully, enriching the positive impact of the practice.

Expanding Your Gratitude Practice

For a deeper experience, you can try additional gratitude exercises:

- **Gratitude Meditation**: Spend a few minutes in quiet reflection, focusing on the people, experiences, or things you're thankful for. Visualize each one, allowing yourself to feel warmth and appreciation for each blessing.
- **Gratitude Letters**: Write a short letter to someone you appreciate, expressing your gratitude. You don't have to send it; simply writing it down helps deepen your sense of thankfulness.

- **Gratitude Jar**: Keep a small jar where you add a note each day with something you're grateful for. Over time, you'll create a collection of memories and positive moments that you can revisit whenever you need a boost.

Practicing Gratitude in Difficult Times

Gratitude is especially powerful during challenging moments. When things aren't going as planned or life feels overwhelming, gratitude can act as an anchor. On hard days, focus on small, grounding things you might usually take for granted—the comfort of your bed, a friendly smile, or simply your own resilience in facing the day. Practicing gratitude during tough times helps build resilience and reminds you of the strength and support you have within and around you.

Reflection Exercise

Take a few minutes to answer these questions in your journal, allowing yourself to explore how gratitude is shifting your mindset:

- **How do I feel after practicing gratitude today?**
- **What difference do I notice in my mood or outlook after reflecting on what I'm grateful for?**
- **How can I incorporate gratitude more deeply into my daily life?**

Gratitude Affirmations

To reinforce your gratitude practice, try using these affirmations to encourage a grateful mindset:

- "I am grateful for the abundance in my life, both seen and unseen."
- "I choose to focus on the good and appreciate the blessings around me."
- "Every day, I discover new things to be grateful for."

A Simple Daily Gratitude Routine

1. **Morning**: Start your day by mentally noting one thing you're grateful for as you wake up. It could be something as simple as the opportunity to start fresh or a peaceful night's sleep.
2. **Throughout the Day**: When something positive happens, pause for a moment to acknowledge it with gratitude, no matter how small it may seem.

3. **Evening**: In your journal, write down three things you're grateful for that day. Reflect on each one, savoring the positive feelings they bring.

Day 12: Creating a Physical Space for Productivity and Calm

Today's focus is on the impact of your **physical environment**—how it influences your productivity, focus, and sense of calm. The spaces where we work, relax, and reflect are extensions of our inner world, and when these spaces are thoughtfully designed, they can support both our goals and well-being. A productive, calming environment doesn't require expensive decor or complicated changes; often, a few intentional adjustments can transform a space into a place that fosters focus, creativity, and peace.

Whether it's a corner in your room, a dedicated office, or even a small table, creating a space that aligns with your intentions can be incredibly grounding. Today, we'll explore how to design a space that feels welcoming, organized, and inspiring, helping you cultivate productivity and calm with greater ease.

Why Your Environment Matters

Research shows that our surroundings significantly impact our mental and emotional state. A cluttered, chaotic space can lead to stress and distraction, while an organized, aesthetically pleasing environment supports focus and relaxation. By mindfully designing a physical space, you're creating a supportive environment that encourages you to work with clarity, manage stress, and feel at ease.

Steps to Create a Space for Productivity and Calm

Creating a productive, calming space is about more than organization—it's about crafting an environment that feels intentional, inspiring, and supportive. Here's a step-by-step guide to designing a space that fosters both focus and tranquility:

1. **Choose a Dedicated Area**:
   o Designate a specific area for your productive and reflective activities. This could be a desk, a corner of a room, or even a particular chair. By assigning a space for focused work or relaxation, you signal to your brain that this is a place of purpose.
2. **Clear Out Clutter**:

- Start by decluttering the space. Remove items that don't serve a purpose or bring you joy. Clutter can be distracting and overwhelming, so aim to keep only what you need or find meaningful in this area. A clear space promotes a clear mind.

3. **Incorporate Natural Elements**:
   - Adding natural elements, like plants or flowers, can boost your mood and reduce stress. Natural light is ideal, but if your space lacks it, try adding soft lighting to create a warm, calming ambiance. If possible, set up near a window to enjoy sunlight and fresh air.

4. **Organize Essentials**:
   - Keep essential items within reach, such as notebooks, pens, or any tools you need for work or reflection. Use trays, drawers, or small organizers to keep these items tidy. An organized space minimizes distractions and saves you time looking for things, enhancing productivity.

5. **Add a Touch of Inspiration**:
   - Include personal touches that inspire you, such as a favorite book, a quote, or a vision board. Choose items that remind you of your goals or make you feel motivated. Surrounding yourself with meaningful objects can enhance your sense of purpose and keep you inspired.

6. **Create a Comfortable Setup**:
   - Comfort is key for focus. Choose a supportive chair and consider adding a cushion or blanket for added coziness. If you'll be working for extended periods, make sure your setup is ergonomically friendly to reduce physical strain.

7. **Set a Calming Tone**:
   - To promote a sense of calm, consider adding elements like a candle, essential oil diffuser, or soft music. Scents like lavender, eucalyptus, or chamomile can be soothing, while calming sounds or gentle background music can create an atmosphere of tranquility.

Design Ideas for a Productive and Calm Space

Here are some ideas for transforming your space into a supportive environment for both productivity and relaxation:

- **The Minimalist Desk**: Keep only the essentials—your computer, a notebook, a pen, and a plant. This setup minimizes distractions and promotes focus.
- **The Cozy Corner**: Add a comfortable chair, a small side table, and a cozy blanket. Use this space for journaling, reading, or quiet reflection.
- **The Inspiration Nook**: Set up a vision board, a few favorite books, and a candle. Surround yourself with images and words that remind you of your goals and values.
- **The Green Oasis**: Bring in a few plants or flowers to create a connection with nature. Studies show that plants reduce stress and increase productivity, making this a great option for any workspace.

Daily Rituals for Your Space

Once your space is set up, create small rituals to keep it feeling fresh and inviting:

- **Morning Setup**: Start each day by tidying your space, lighting a candle, or playing calming music to set a positive tone.
- **Midday Reset**: Take a few minutes during the day to declutter or rearrange items, ensuring your space stays organized and inspiring.
- **Evening Wind-Down**: Clear your desk or area at the end of the day. This small act of closure helps you mentally "close" the day, leaving the space ready for a fresh start tomorrow.

Reflection Exercise

In your journal, take a moment to answer these questions:

- **How does my environment make me feel? Does it support my focus and peace?**
- **What small changes could I make to enhance my space's calm and productivity?**
- **What items bring me joy and motivation, and how can I incorporate them into my space?**

Tips for Maintaining a Productive and Calming Space

1. **Keep It Simple**: Less is often more. Prioritize simplicity and purpose over adding too many decorative items.
2. **Make It Personal**: Choose items that resonate with you personally. Your space should feel unique and aligned with your tastes and goals.
3. **Refresh Regularly**: Periodically declutter and update your space to keep it feeling fresh. A small change, like a new plant or rearranging furniture, can make the area feel revitalized.

Day 13: Breaking Down Big Goals into Small, Achievable Steps

Today's focus is on the art of **goal setting**—specifically, transforming big goals into manageable, achievable steps. Big dreams and goals can feel inspiring, yet they can also feel overwhelming, causing us to freeze or procrastinate because we don't know where to start. By breaking down your big goals into smaller, actionable steps, you make the path forward clearer, more motivating, and less intimidating. Small steps give you tangible progress to celebrate along the way, helping you stay engaged and committed.

When we approach big goals with a step-by-step mindset, each small action builds momentum, confidence, and clarity. You're not only working toward a future achievement; you're actively shaping your journey in the present.

Why Breaking Down Goals Matters

Big goals are often multifaceted, requiring a series of actions, adjustments, and even setbacks along the way. By breaking down your goals, you're giving yourself a clear road map, ensuring that each step feels manageable and achievable. Research shows that we're more likely to reach our goals when we divide them into specific, attainable steps. Each small win provides a sense of accomplishment, which releases dopamine in the brain, reinforcing your motivation to continue.

A step-by-step approach also makes it easier to adjust if needed. If one path isn't working, you can pivot without feeling lost, focusing instead on the next small, actionable item.

Steps to Break Down Big Goals

To make your big goals feel achievable, let's walk through a process to break them down into clear, manageable steps:

1. **Define Your Goal Clearly**:
   o Start by writing down your big goal as clearly and specifically as possible. Instead of vague goals like "I want to be healthier," specify "I want to improve my physical fitness and energy levels."
2. **Identify Key Milestones**:

o Break down your goal into major milestones. Think of milestones as "mini-goals" or markers of progress along the way. For example, if your goal is to write a book, a milestone could be "complete the first draft" or "research and outline each chapter."

3. **List Actionable Steps for Each Milestone**:
   o For each milestone, list specific actions you need to take. These should be small, concrete tasks that can be completed in a short time frame. For instance, if your milestone is to complete the first draft of a book, actionable steps could include "write 500 words per day" or "outline Chapter 1."

4. **Set a Timeline**:
   o Assign a realistic deadline to each milestone and action step. Setting a timeframe keeps you accountable, but be flexible enough to adjust as needed. Breaking down a goal into a weekly or monthly timeline can make it feel manageable and encourage steady progress.

5. **Focus on One Step at a Time**:
   o Avoid the urge to tackle multiple steps at once. Instead, focus on completing one action at a time. This keeps you present and reduces overwhelm. Each small step is a part of the bigger picture, so trust that each action is bringing you closer to your goal.

Example: Breaking Down a Big Goal

Let's say your big goal is to "Run a marathon in six months." Here's how you might break it down:

- **Milestone 1**: Build a Base Level of Fitness (First 4 Weeks)
  o Step 1: Start with a 20-minute jog, 3 times a week.
  o Step 2: Increase jog time by 5 minutes each week.
  o Step 3: Add a weekend 30-minute walk or hike for endurance.
- **Milestone 2**: Increase Weekly Distance (Weeks 5–12)
  o Step 1: Follow a structured training plan (e.g., increase running distance by 10% each week).

- Step 2: Add one long run each weekend, starting with 5 miles.
- Step 3: Incorporate cross-training (cycling or swimming) for strength.
- **Milestone 3**: Focus on Marathon-Specific Training (Weeks 13–24)
  - Step 1: Practice running at marathon pace on shorter runs.
  - Step 2: Gradually extend long runs to reach 18–20 miles.
  - Step 3: Work with a coach or running group for feedback and motivation.

By breaking down the goal into milestones and steps, the marathon doesn't feel like an impossible leap; instead, it's a series of achievable actions that build on each other.

Tips for Staying on Track

1. **Celebrate Small Wins**: Each completed step is a small victory. Celebrate these moments with small rewards or simple recognition, acknowledging the progress you're making.
2. **Track Your Progress**: Use a journal, planner, or app to track each completed step. Visual progress can be a powerful motivator, reminding you of how far you've come.
3. **Stay Flexible**: Life may bring changes to your plans, and that's okay. Adjust timelines or steps as needed, but keep moving forward with small, consistent actions.
4. **Reflect Regularly**: Take time each week or month to review your progress and adjust any steps if needed. Reflection helps you stay connected to your "why" and adapt your approach if needed.

Reflection Exercise

In your journal, break down one of your big goals using the steps above. Reflect on the following prompts:

- **What milestones will help me track my progress toward this goal?**
- **What small, actionable steps can I start with to build momentum?**

—

- **How can I celebrate my progress as I reach each milestone?**

Daily Affirmations for Motivation

To keep your mindset aligned with your goals, try using these affirmations:

- "Each small step I take brings me closer to my goals."
- "I have the patience and perseverance to achieve my dreams."
- "Every action I take is a step forward on my journey."

Embracing the Journey

Remember, big goals are achieved through the consistent, small steps we take each day. The path may have ups and downs, but by focusing on one step at a time, you're building both momentum and resilience. Embrace each small achievement, and trust that every step is bringing you closer to the person you want to become and the life you want to create. Each action, no matter how small, is a part of your journey—and with each step, you're making your goals a reality.

Day 14: Reflecting on Week 2 – Tracking Progress and Adjustments

Congratulations on completing your second week of this journey! This week, you focused on building core habits that support your goals and well-being, from creating a morning ritual to setting up a productive space and breaking down big goals into achievable steps. Today is a time to pause, reflect on your progress, and assess any adjustments that might help you move forward with clarity and confidence.

Reflection is a powerful tool in personal growth. It allows you to celebrate the wins, acknowledge challenges, and refine your approach. As you reflect on the past week, you'll gain valuable insights into what's working well and where you can make small tweaks to stay on track with your goals. This intentional practice of review and adjustment helps you stay connected to your purpose and build momentum as you continue your journey.

The Importance of Reflection

Regular reflection reinforces your commitment to growth and gives you the opportunity to celebrate your efforts, no matter how small. By taking a step back to look at your progress, you're giving yourself a clear perspective on what you've achieved and how you're feeling about the journey so far. Reflection isn't just about tracking successes; it's also about learning from the obstacles and using those lessons to refine your approach.

As you reflect, remember that growth is a process, not a destination. Every step you take—no matter how big or small—is a part of your journey, and each experience provides valuable feedback for the path ahead.

Reflecting on Your Progress

Take a few moments to consider your experiences from the past week. Use the following prompts to guide your reflection and capture your insights:

1. **What are the Small Wins I'm Proud Of?**

o Reflect on the progress you've made, whether it's a new habit you've formed, a productive morning ritual, or breaking down a big goal. Celebrate these small victories—they are the building blocks of lasting change.

2. **What Challenges Did I Encounter?**
   o Acknowledge any difficulties you faced, such as moments of doubt, procrastination, or a struggle to stick with a habit. Don't view these as setbacks; instead, see them as opportunities to learn more about yourself and refine your approach.

3. **How Have My New Habits Impacted Me?**
   o Think about the impact of the routines and habits you've put in place. Do you feel more focused, calm, or motivated? Noticing the positive changes, however subtle, reinforces the value of your efforts and helps you stay committed.

4. **What Adjustments Can I Make?**
   o Identify any areas where you'd like to make small adjustments. Perhaps your morning ritual could use a different activity, or your goals would benefit from smaller, more specific steps. These tweaks help keep your journey aligned with your needs and goals.

5. **What Am I Grateful For on This Journey?**
   o Gratitude helps anchor you in the present moment, reminding you of the joy and growth in each step. Consider the support you've received, the resilience you've shown, or the self-discoveries you've made.

Making Adjustments for the Coming Week

Based on your reflections, consider any adjustments you'd like to make as you move into the next week. These could be small shifts in your routines, a change in your environment, or even a renewed focus on a particular goal. The goal isn't to overhaul everything but to make thoughtful tweaks that support your continued growth.

1. **Adjust Your Rituals if Needed**:

o   If you find that your morning or evening routine isn't quite working, experiment with different activities or timings. Sometimes, a small change, like adding a quick stretch or a moment of stillness, can make your routine feel more aligned.

2. **Reassess Your Steps**:
   o   If a goal feels overwhelming or progress feels slow, consider breaking it down into even smaller steps. The easier each action feels, the more likely you are to take it consistently.

3. **Address Any Obstacles**:
   o   Think about any specific challenges you faced and plan for how to handle them in the future. If procrastination was an issue, for example, try setting a timer for short work intervals or creating a reward system for completing tasks.

4. **Recommit to Your Intentions**:
   o   Take a moment to reconnect with the intentions you set at the beginning of this journey. Remind yourself why this work matters to you and envision how your efforts are bringing you closer to the life you want.

Reflection Exercise

In your journal, take some time to write out your reflections and any adjustments you'd like to make. Answer the following questions to capture your insights and plan for the week ahead:

- **What progress am I most proud of from this week?**
- **What challenges did I encounter, and what did I learn from them?**
- **What adjustments can I make to stay aligned with my goals?**
- **How has this journey been impacting my mindset and daily life?**
- **What intentions do I want to carry forward into the next week?**

Celebrating Your Progress

Every small step forward deserves recognition. Give yourself credit for the commitment and effort you've shown, regardless of the pace or size of each win. Growth is a journey, and by celebrating each step, you reinforce the positive changes you're making.

Consider a small reward or gesture to celebrate the end of this week. It could be a relaxing activity, a moment of gratitude, or a simple acknowledgment of your achievements. Let this celebration be a reminder of how far you've come and a motivation for the steps still ahead.

Week 3: Enhancing Productivity and Focus

Day 15: Time Management Essentials – Identifying Priorities

Today's focus is on **time management** and, specifically, identifying your priorities—the cornerstone of effective time management. Time is one of our most precious resources, yet it's easy to feel that there's never quite enough of it. By learning to identify and prioritize what truly matters, you can make the most of each day, channeling your energy into activities that support your goals, well-being, and personal growth.

Effective time management isn't about cramming more tasks into your day; it's about thoughtfully choosing how to spend your time. When you focus on high-priority activities, you create space for growth, reduce stress, and find greater satisfaction in the work you accomplish. Today, we'll explore essential strategies to help you clarify your priorities, making it easier to allocate time to the things that align with your values and goals.

Why Identifying Priorities Matters

Without clear priorities, it's easy to get swept up in low-impact tasks or distractions, leaving us feeling busy but unfulfilled. When we prioritize intentionally, we're directing our energy toward what truly adds value to our lives, whether that's personal goals, relationships, or self-care. By identifying priorities, you're setting the foundation for a balanced, productive, and purpose-driven life.

Understanding your priorities also makes it easier to say "no" to tasks that don't align with your goals, freeing up time for what truly matters.

Steps to Identify and Prioritize Your Goals

To make the most of your time, start by clarifying your most important goals and commitments. Here's a step-by-step guide to help you identify and prioritize your tasks effectively:

---

1. **Define Your Core Values and Long-Term Goals**:
   o Think about the values and goals that guide your life. What matters most to you? Is it personal growth, career success, relationships, or health? Defining your core values gives you a framework for identifying tasks that align with what truly matters.
   o For example, if personal growth is a top value, prioritizing activities that promote learning or self-reflection will be essential.
2. **Identify Your Top Priorities for This Season**:
   o Your priorities may shift depending on where you are in life. Consider the current season you're in and what needs the most attention. If you're working on a major project, that may take precedence; if you're focused on health, prioritize activities that support well-being.
   o List your top 3–5 priorities for this season. This helps create focus and prevents overcommitment.
3. **Break Down Priorities into Actionable Tasks**:
   o Once you've identified your priorities, break them down into specific tasks or actions. For example, if "improve physical health" is a priority, actionable tasks might include scheduling workouts, planning healthy meals, or getting enough sleep.
   o Defining concrete tasks helps you see exactly what needs to be done and reduces overwhelm.
4. **Use the Eisenhower Matrix to Organize Tasks**:
   o The Eisenhower Matrix is a tool that helps you categorize tasks by urgency and importance. It consists of four quadrants:
      ▪ **Important and Urgent**: Tasks that need immediate attention. Prioritize these first.
      ▪ **Important but Not Urgent**: Tasks that are significant but don't require immediate action (e.g., planning, long-term goals). These are often the most impactful and should be scheduled regularly.

- **Not Important but Urgent**: Tasks that need attention but don't contribute to your core goals (e.g., certain emails or minor requests). Delegate these when possible.
- **Not Important and Not Urgent**: Low-impact tasks or distractions (e.g., social media scrolling). Limit these activities to preserve time for higher priorities.

5. **Establish Daily "Top Three" Priorities**:
   - Each morning, set three high-priority tasks that you intend to complete by the end of the day. These should be aligned with your main goals and reflect the actions that bring the most value.
   - Focusing on just three tasks prevents overwhelm and keeps you moving forward on what matters most.

Example: Identifying Priorities for a Productive Week

Let's say your top priority for the month is to write a book. Here's how you might apply these steps:

- **Priority**: Complete the book outline by the end of the month.
  - **Important and Urgent Tasks**: Finalize research, outline first two chapters.
  - **Important but Not Urgent Tasks**: Set aside daily writing time, create a list of chapter topics.
  - **Not Important but Urgent Tasks**: Responding to unrelated emails or requests (limit these during focused writing time).
  - **Not Important and Not Urgent Tasks**: Limit social media or non-related activities during writing hours.

By categorizing tasks in this way, you're able to focus more deeply on what drives your goals while reducing distractions.

Tips for Staying Focused on Priorities

1. **Review Your Priorities Weekly**: At the start or end of each week, revisit your priorities and adjust as needed. A weekly review keeps you on track and gives you the flexibility to respond to changes.

2. **Set Boundaries**: Protect your high-priority time by setting boundaries, both with yourself and others. For example, set a time block for focused work and let others know you're unavailable during this time.
3. **Limit Multitasking**: Focus on one priority task at a time. Multitasking can dilute your attention and reduce effectiveness. Give each task your full attention, and you'll accomplish more with less stress.
4. **Celebrate Progress**: Recognize and celebrate your accomplishments, even the small ones. Acknowledging progress reinforces motivation and reminds you of the value of prioritizing.

Reflection Exercise

In your journal, take some time to reflect on the following prompts to gain clarity on your current priorities:

- **What are my top 3–5 priorities this season, and why are they important to me?**
- **How can I break down my priorities into actionable steps that fit into my daily schedule?**
- **What tasks could I let go of or delegate to free up time for my main priorities?**

Affirmations for Time Management

To keep your mindset focused on productivity and intentional action, use these affirmations:

- "I prioritize tasks that align with my goals and values."
- "My time is precious, and I use it wisely."
- "I am focused, intentional, and committed to my priorities."

Moving Forward with Clarity and Purpose

By identifying and focusing on your priorities, you're creating a roadmap for meaningful action. Each day, when you focus on what matters most, you're building a life that aligns with your goals and values. Remember, managing your time is about making conscious choices that support your well-being and growth. Embrace each small, focused step forward as a powerful action toward your vision, and let your priorities guide you on this path of purpose and fulfillment.

Day 16: The Power of Deep Work – Minimizing Distractions

Today's focus is on **deep work**—the ability to concentrate intensely on a demanding task without interruption. Deep work is about diving fully into a single task, free from distractions, allowing you to produce high-quality work efficiently and creatively. In a world filled with constant notifications and multitasking, deep work has become a rare but invaluable skill. By learning to minimize distractions and cultivate focused time, you're setting yourself up for breakthroughs in productivity, creativity, and personal satisfaction.

Deep work isn't just about getting more done; it's about working on the things that matter most with intention and depth. When you can maintain uninterrupted focus, even for short periods, you build momentum, clarity, and the satisfaction that comes from truly engaging with your goals.

The Benefits of Deep Work

Engaging in deep work has a profound impact on your ability to learn, create, and complete complex tasks. Research shows that deep focus enhances cognitive performance, making it easier to solve problems and produce high-quality work in less time. Deep work also reduces stress because you're dedicating focused energy to priority tasks, reducing the anxiety that comes from juggling multiple tasks or battling distractions.

In essence, deep work helps you do more of what truly matters, making each session of focused work an investment in both your productivity and well-being.

Strategies for Minimizing Distractions and Cultivating Deep Work

Deep work requires commitment and an environment that supports focus. Here's a step-by-step guide to help you reduce distractions and get into a deep work state:

1. **Designate Time Blocks for Deep Work**:

- o Schedule specific blocks of time each day or week dedicated to deep work. These time blocks don't need to be long—start with 30–60 minutes if you're new to deep work. The key is to protect this time and treat it as a priority.
- o Avoid scheduling meetings or other tasks during these blocks to ensure you have uninterrupted focus.

2. **Create a Distraction-Free Environment**:
   - o Set up a workspace where distractions are minimized. Put away unnecessary items, turn off notifications on your devices, and close any tabs or apps not related to your work.
   - o If you work from home or in a shared space, communicate to others that you're in a deep work session to reduce interruptions.

3. **Use the Pomodoro Technique**:
   - o The Pomodoro Technique involves working in focused intervals, usually 25–30 minutes, followed by a short break. This method can help you build focus and train your mind to work deeply in short bursts.
   - o Start with one or two Pomodoro intervals and gradually increase your focus duration as you build your deep work muscles.

4. **Set Clear Goals for Each Session**:
   - o Before starting your deep work session, set a specific goal. Instead of "work on project," try "complete the outline for Chapter 3" or "write 500 words." Clear goals give your mind direction and make it easier to stay focused.
   - o At the end of each session, reflect on what you've accomplished. This helps reinforce the value of deep work and gives you a sense of achievement.

5. **Manage Digital Distractions**:
   - o Turn off notifications on your phone and computer. Consider using tools like "Do Not Disturb" mode or website blockers to prevent access to distracting sites during deep work.

- o If you're easily tempted to check your phone, place it out of sight or in another room to keep your focus on the task at hand.

6. **Embrace "Monotasking"**:
   - o Deep work thrives on monotasking, or focusing on a single task at a time. Avoid switching between tasks, as each switch costs mental energy and disrupts your focus.
   - o Challenge yourself to stay on one task for the duration of your deep work block, allowing your mind to fully engage with the work at hand.
7. **Practice Mindful Focus**:
   - o If you notice your mind wandering, gently bring your attention back to the task. Deep work requires mental discipline, and with practice, you'll find it easier to maintain focus for longer periods.
   - o Consider taking a few deep breaths before starting each session to calm your mind and prepare for focused work.

Building Your Deep Work Routine

Deep work is a skill that strengthens with practice. Here's a sample routine to help you integrate deep work into your daily life:

1. **Start Small**: Begin with a 30-minute deep work block each day. Gradually increase the time as your ability to focus strengthens.
2. **Set a Weekly Goal**: Determine one or two priority projects where deep work will have the most impact. Set goals that you'll focus on during your deep work sessions, and track your progress each week.
3. **Create a Ritual for Deep Work**: Develop a short routine before each session, such as stretching, clearing your desk, or taking a few deep breaths. This ritual signals to your mind that it's time to focus.
4. **End with Reflection**: At the end of each deep work session, write down what you accomplished and any insights you gained. Reflecting on your progress reinforces the benefits of deep work and keeps you motivated.

Daily Reflection Exercise

In your journal, reflect on the following prompts to deepen your understanding of deep work and its impact on your goals:

- **What projects or tasks would benefit most from deep work sessions?**
- **What distractions tend to pull me away from focused work, and how can I manage them?**
- **How do I feel after a deep work session? Do I notice a difference in my productivity or satisfaction?**

Affirmations for Focus and Deep Work

To keep your mind centered on focus and intention, try using these affirmations:

- "I am focused, disciplined, and committed to my goals."
- "My time and attention are valuable, and I use them wisely."
- "I embrace deep work to create meaningful progress."

Moving Forward with Deep Work

By prioritizing deep work, you're cultivating a skill that can transform your productivity and fulfillment. Each time you dedicate focused, uninterrupted time to a task, you're not only making meaningful progress but also strengthening your ability to concentrate deeply—a skill that benefits every area of life. Embrace this time as a powerful investment in your goals, and let each deep work session be a reminder of your commitment to creating work that matters.

With practice, deep work will become a natural part of your routine, bringing greater clarity, productivity, and purpose to your journey.

Day 17: Learning to Say No – Creating Space for What Matters

Today's focus is on the powerful skill of **saying no**—a simple but essential tool for protecting your time, energy, and priorities. In a world that often encourages us to say yes to every opportunity, request, and invitation, learning to say no can feel challenging. But by consciously choosing where to invest your energy, you're creating space for what truly matters, allowing you to focus on the people, projects, and experiences that align with your goals and values.

Saying no isn't about rejecting others; it's about affirming your own needs and boundaries. Each time you say no to something that doesn't align with your priorities, you're saying yes to what does, freeing up time for growth, well-being, and fulfillment.

Why Learning to Say No Matters

When we overcommit or agree to things that don't resonate with us, we spread ourselves too thin, leaving less energy for what's truly important. Saying no allows us to be more intentional with our time and reduces stress by creating boundaries that protect our mental and emotional health. Research shows that those who can set boundaries experience higher levels of satisfaction and productivity, as they have the mental space to focus on what brings them purpose and joy.

Saying no can feel uncomfortable at first, especially if you're worried about disappointing others. However, each time you practice, you strengthen your ability to prioritize your own needs and values, fostering self-respect and a deeper connection to what matters most.

Steps to Start Saying No with Confidence

Learning to say no is a skill that becomes easier with practice. Here's a guide to help you approach it with confidence and clarity:

1. **Clarify Your Priorities and Values**:

o   Take a moment to identify your top priorities and values. When you're clear on what matters to you, it's easier to recognize which requests align with those priorities and which don't. If family, personal growth, or a specific project is a priority, anything that detracts from these may be a candidate for a respectful no.

2. **Pause Before Responding**:
   o   When a request or invitation comes your way, avoid committing immediately. Take a brief pause to consider whether it aligns with your priorities. This moment of reflection gives you the space to decide thoughtfully rather than out of habit or obligation.

3. **Use Simple, Respectful Language**:
   o   A direct but kind approach makes it easier to say no without overexplaining. Simple phrases like "I appreciate the offer, but I'm unable to commit at this time" or "Thank you for thinking of me, but I'll have to pass" are effective and respectful. You don't need to provide detailed reasons—just a courteous response that respects both you and the other person.

4. **Practice Saying No to Small Requests**:
   o   If saying no feels intimidating, start with smaller requests, like declining a casual invitation or a low-priority task. Practicing in lower-stakes situations builds confidence, making it easier to say no in situations that matter more.

5. **Remind Yourself of the Bigger Picture**:
   o   Each time you say no to something that doesn't align with your goals, you're making room for something that does. Remind yourself of the bigger picture: the meaningful work, relationships, and personal well-being that you're prioritizing. This perspective shift helps reduce any guilt and reinforces the value of your decision.

6. **Stay Firm but Compassionate**:

    o   If someone tries to persuade you to reconsider, calmly reiterate your decision. Acknowledge their request but stay committed to your choice. For example, "I understand this is important to you, but I have to prioritize other commitments at the moment."

Examples of Saying No with Grace

Learning to say no doesn't mean being dismissive. Here are a few examples to help you decline with kindness and respect:

- **Request to Take on Extra Work**: "Thank you for considering me for this project. Right now, I'm focusing on my current responsibilities, so I won't be able to take on additional tasks."
- **Invitation to an Event**: "I appreciate the invitation, but I'll have to decline. I hope it's a wonderful event, and thank you for including me."
- **Helping with a Favor**: "I'd love to help, but I'm currently managing a lot on my plate. I hope you find the support you need."

By responding with sincerity and respect, you're honoring both your boundaries and the other person's request.

Benefits of Saying No

Each time you say no to something that doesn't align with your priorities, you're affirming your commitment to your own well-being. The benefits of saying no extend beyond time management—they include:

- **Reduced Stress and Overwhelm**: By focusing on fewer commitments, you're reducing the mental clutter that can lead to stress and fatigue.
- **Increased Quality in Your Work and Relationships**: When you're selective with your time, you can dedicate more energy to the people and projects that mean the most to you.
- **Greater Alignment with Your Goals**: Saying no allows you to make progress on the goals that truly matter, supporting a life that reflects your values.

Daily Reflection Exercise

In your journal, take some time to reflect on these questions to gain clarity on your boundaries and priorities:

- **What are my top three priorities, and how do I want to protect time for them?**
- **Are there any recent commitments that don't align with my values?**
- **How would my life change if I learned to say no more often?**

Affirmations for Setting Boundaries

Use these affirmations to strengthen your resolve to prioritize what matters most:

- "I honor my time and energy by saying no to what doesn't serve me."
- "I create space for what matters by respectfully setting boundaries."
- "Saying no allows me to focus on my goals and values."

Moving Forward with Intention and Boundaries

Learning to say no is a powerful act of self-respect. By setting boundaries around your time and energy, you're not only creating space for your priorities—you're also modeling healthy boundaries for others. Each time you choose to say no to what doesn't serve you, you're creating a life that aligns with your vision, values, and goals.

Embrace this skill as a practice, recognizing that each no is a step toward a more balanced, intentional life. As you continue your journey, let your choices reflect the person you're becoming, someone who knows the value of their time and makes space for what truly matters.

Day 18: Techniques for Overcoming Procrastination

Today's focus is on **overcoming procrastination**—a common hurdle that can prevent us from taking action on our goals. Procrastination is more than a simple delay; it's a pattern of avoiding tasks that can leave us feeling stuck, overwhelmed, or guilty. By understanding why we procrastinate and implementing techniques to overcome it, we can build momentum and make steady progress toward our goals with confidence and clarity.

Procrastination often happens when we feel a task is too challenging, uninteresting, or anxiety-inducing. But with the right strategies, we can break this cycle, approach tasks with a sense of control, and even find joy in the process of taking action. Today, we'll explore practical techniques to help you move forward, one step at a time.

Understanding Procrastination: Why We Delay

Before diving into techniques, it's helpful to understand why procrastination happens. Here are a few common reasons:

1. **Fear of Failure**: We may procrastinate when we're worried about not meeting expectations or making mistakes.
2. **Task Overwhelm**: When a task feels too big or complex, it's easy to put it off because we don't know where to start.
3. **Perfectionism**: Wanting everything to be perfect can lead to delays, as we might feel we're never "ready" to begin.
4. **Lack of Motivation**: If a task doesn't feel meaningful or rewarding, we may procrastinate because it lacks personal value or excitement.

Understanding your reasons for procrastination helps you choose techniques that address the root cause, making it easier to move forward.

Techniques for Overcoming Procrastination

Overcoming procrastination requires a blend of practical strategies and mindset shifts. Here are some effective techniques to help you take action, no matter the task:

1. **Break Tasks into Small Steps**:
   o When a task feels overwhelming, break it down into smaller, manageable steps. Instead of tackling an entire project at once, focus on just the first step.

---

o For example, if you're writing a report, start by simply gathering your notes. Once you've completed that small step, it's easier to move on to the next.

2. **Use the "Two-Minute Rule"**:
   o If a task takes less than two minutes, do it immediately. This rule helps you complete minor tasks quickly rather than letting them build up.
   o For larger tasks, start with just two minutes. Often, starting is the hardest part, and once you begin, you'll find it easier to keep going.

3. **Set a Timer (Pomodoro Technique)**:
   o The Pomodoro Technique involves working for a set time, usually 25 minutes, followed by a short break. Set a timer, work with focus until it rings, and then reward yourself with a five-minute pause.
   o This method helps you overcome the initial resistance to starting, making tasks feel more approachable and preventing burnout.

4. **Visualize the End Result**:
   o Take a moment to picture how you'll feel once the task is complete. Visualizing the positive outcome can help you connect with the benefits of finishing, boosting motivation and creating a sense of urgency.
   o Imagine the relief, satisfaction, or pride you'll experience, and let that feeling motivate you to begin.

5. **Practice Self-Compassion**:
   o Procrastination often comes with self-criticism, which can make it harder to get started. Replace negative self-talk with self-compassion. Remind yourself that everyone procrastinates occasionally and that each step forward is progress, no matter how small.
   o Be gentle with yourself, and celebrate any effort you make, even if it's just a small one.

6. **Create a Reward System**:

- Give yourself a reward for completing tasks, especially if they're challenging or unappealing. The reward doesn't have to be big; it could be a short walk, a treat, or a quick break to do something you enjoy.
- Creating small incentives gives you something to look forward to, making tasks feel more achievable and enjoyable.

7. **Eliminate Distractions**:
   - Set up a workspace that minimizes distractions. Turn off notifications, close unrelated tabs, and put your phone out of sight. If you're prone to digital distractions, consider using apps that block certain websites during work sessions.
   - A focused environment makes it easier to maintain your concentration and stay on task.

8. **Commit to "Just Five Minutes"**:
   - Tell yourself you'll work on the task for just five minutes. Often, the hardest part is simply starting, and once you begin, you may find it easier to keep going.
   - This technique reduces the pressure to complete the entire task, allowing you to ease into it and gain momentum naturally.

Example: Applying These Techniques to a Task

Let's say you have a big presentation coming up, and you've been procrastinating on preparing it. Here's how you might apply these techniques:

1. **Break it Down**: Start by creating an outline. Next, gather information for each section. Finally, work on the slides one by one.
2. **Set a Timer**: Use the Pomodoro Technique to work on the presentation in 25-minute intervals.
3. **Visualize Completion**: Picture yourself confidently delivering the presentation and receiving positive feedback.
4. **Create a Reward**: Plan a small reward after each work session, such as a cup of tea or a few minutes of relaxation.

By approaching the task with these techniques, you make it feel manageable and enjoyable rather than overwhelming.

Reflection Exercise

In your journal, take a few moments to reflect on the following questions:

- **What tasks have I been putting off, and why?**
- **Which technique(s) would be most helpful in tackling these tasks?**
- **How do I feel after using these techniques to take a small step forward?**

Affirmations to Overcome Procrastination

Affirmations can help reframe your mindset and reduce resistance to starting tasks. Try using these affirmations to build motivation:

- "I take small steps forward with confidence and ease."
- "I am capable of completing tasks, one step at a time."
- "I approach each task with focus and commitment."

Moving Forward with Action and Purpose

Overcoming procrastination is about breaking the cycle of avoidance and building a habit of action. By using these techniques, you're not only taking steps toward your goals but also building self-trust and confidence. Remember, the journey to progress often begins with just one small action. Embrace each step, and know that every effort counts as a part of your growth.

Let today mark a fresh start in your relationship with tasks and goals. Approach each one with patience, curiosity, and the knowledge that you have the power to move forward, no matter how challenging the path may seem.

Day 19: The Pomodoro Technique – Maximizing Work Intervals

Today's focus is on a time-management method designed to enhance focus and productivity: the **Pomodoro Technique**. Named after the Italian word for "tomato" (inspired by a tomato-shaped kitchen timer), the Pomodoro Technique is a simple yet powerful approach that breaks work into focused intervals, separated by short breaks. This technique not only makes tasks feel more manageable but also helps you maintain energy and motivation over extended periods.

With the Pomodoro Technique, you work in **bursts of concentrated effort**, typically 25 minutes, followed by a short break. These structured intervals make it easier to dive deep into tasks without feeling overwhelmed, helping you maximize productivity, reduce mental fatigue, and make steady progress on your goals.

Why the Pomodoro Technique Works

Our brains are wired to thrive with focused work followed by periods of rest. The Pomodoro Technique taps into this natural rhythm, preventing burnout by giving your mind a moment to recharge after each interval. This method encourages you to stay fully present with one task at a time, minimizing distractions and promoting "deep work." Additionally, breaking work into intervals can make daunting tasks feel more approachable, turning each session into a manageable, achievable goal.

Research shows that short, focused bursts of work can improve concentration and productivity, while regular breaks help maintain energy levels, allowing you to work longer and more effectively without sacrificing quality.

How to Use the Pomodoro Technique

The Pomodoro Technique is straightforward and easy to implement. Here's a step-by-step guide to help you get started and make the most of each work interval:

1. **Choose a Task**:
   o Select a task you want to work on. It could be a single project, a part of a larger goal, or even a set of small tasks. For best results, try to focus on one task per Pomodoro to maintain concentration and clarity.

2. **Set a Timer for 25 Minutes**:
   - Use a timer to set a strict 25-minute work period. During this time, commit to focusing solely on your chosen task. Avoid any interruptions, and if distractions arise, jot them down to revisit after the Pomodoro session.
3. **Work Without Distractions**:
   - Dive fully into your task, giving it your undivided attention. This time is for deep, focused work, so try to avoid multitasking or switching between tasks.
4. **Take a 5-Minute Break**:
   - When the timer goes off, stop working, even if you're in the middle of something. Use this 5-minute break to step away, stretch, hydrate, or simply rest your mind. These short breaks are essential for maintaining focus and energy.
5. **Repeat the Process**:
   - After your 5-minute break, start another 25-minute Pomodoro session. Aim to complete four Pomodoros, or 25-minute intervals, in a row before taking a longer break.
6. **Take a Longer Break After Four Pomodoros**:
   - Once you've completed four Pomodoro intervals, reward yourself with a longer break, typically 15–30 minutes. Use this time to recharge fully before starting another set of Pomodoros if needed.

Tips for Making the Pomodoro Technique Effective
1. **Minimize Digital Distractions**:
   - Turn off notifications, close unrelated tabs, and put your phone on "Do Not Disturb." If you're tempted to check social media, remind yourself that you'll have a break soon and can catch up then.
2. **Start Small and Build Up**:
   - If 25 minutes feels too long at first, start with shorter intervals, like 15 or 20 minutes, and gradually build up as you get used to the technique.
3. **Batch Small Tasks Together**:

o   If you have several small tasks (like answering emails or making phone calls), batch them together into one Pomodoro session. This helps you handle minor tasks efficiently without disrupting larger blocks of focused time.

4. **Track Your Progress**:
    o   Use a notebook or app to track each completed Pomodoro. Not only does this help you stay motivated, but it also gives you a sense of accomplishment as you see your progress add up.

5. **Adjust Pomodoros for Different Tasks**:
    o   Not all tasks require the same level of focus. For less demanding tasks, you might shorten your Pomodoro intervals or take slightly longer breaks. Customize the technique to suit the nature of each task.

Example: Using the Pomodoro Technique for a Project

Let's say you're working on a report that includes research, writing, and editing. Here's how you might structure your Pomodoros for the day:

1. **Pomodoro 1**: Research and gather key points (25 minutes).
    o   **Break**: Take a 5-minute break to stretch.
2. **Pomodoro 2**: Outline the report structure (25 minutes).
    o   **Break**: Take a 5-minute break to refresh.
3. **Pomodoro 3**: Write the introduction and first section (25 minutes).
    o   **Break**: Take a 5-minute break.
4. **Pomodoro 4**: Continue writing the main content (25 minutes).
    o   **Longer Break**: Take a 15–30-minute break, allowing your mind to rest before continuing.

By dividing your project into Pomodoros, you avoid feeling overwhelmed and maintain steady progress without exhausting your focus.

Reflection Exercise

In your journal, answer these questions to reflect on your experience with the Pomodoro Technique:

- **What tasks benefit most from focused Pomodoro sessions?**
- **How does taking regular breaks impact my energy and concentration?**
- **What changes can I make to better support my deep work using this technique?**

Affirmations for Focus and Productivity

Use these affirmations to reinforce your focus and motivation during each Pomodoro session:

- "I am fully present and focused on one task at a time."
- "I work with intention, knowing breaks help me recharge."
- "I embrace the power of small, focused intervals to achieve my goals."

Moving Forward with the Pomodoro Technique

The Pomodoro Technique is a versatile tool that supports both productivity and well-being. Each Pomodoro session is a reminder that work can be broken down into achievable parts, making large tasks feel more manageable. By working in focused intervals, you're developing a habit of mindful concentration and pacing yourself in a way that sustains energy and motivation.

Embrace this technique as a tool to maximize your time, enjoy each step of your work, and end the day feeling accomplished. Let each Pomodoro bring you closer to your goals, one focused interval at a time.

Day 20: Mastering Energy Management Over Time Management

Today's focus is on a powerful shift in productivity: **energy management** rather than just time management. While time management teaches us how to allocate hours, energy management helps us harness our natural rhythms and reserves to maximize productivity, well-being, and creativity. Mastering energy management is about working with your body and mind to sustain focus, efficiency, and enjoyment throughout the day.

When we prioritize energy over time, we become more intentional about the tasks we choose and the times we choose to tackle them. This approach acknowledges that our energy fluctuates based on physical, mental, and emotional factors, and that understanding these rhythms is key to doing our best work while avoiding burnout.

Why Energy Management Matters

Simply scheduling tasks isn't always enough to accomplish them effectively; how much energy you bring to each task greatly influences the quality of your work. If you've ever felt tired, unmotivated, or overwhelmed despite having time blocked off for work, you know that time alone doesn't guarantee productivity. Energy management allows you to align tasks with your natural highs and lows, making it easier to focus, stay creative, and reduce stress.

By learning to manage energy, you can create a routine that works with your natural patterns, ultimately helping you get more done with less effort and greater satisfaction.

Steps to Master Energy Management

1. **Identify Your Energy Peaks and Valleys**:
   - Start by observing your natural energy levels throughout the day. Many people experience higher energy in the morning, a dip in the afternoon, and a slight boost in the early evening. Track your energy levels for a few days to pinpoint when you're most alert and when you feel sluggish.
   - Use this awareness to structure your day: save high-energy times for focused, demanding work, and

schedule less intensive tasks during low-energy periods.

2. **Prioritize High-Impact Tasks During Peak Energy**:
   - Once you know when you're at your best, prioritize your most important or challenging tasks for these peak energy times. This is when your focus, creativity, and problem-solving skills are strongest, allowing you to tackle complex work more effectively.
   - By matching high-energy periods with high-priority tasks, you're working with your natural rhythms rather than against them.

3. **Take Breaks to Recharge**:
   - Regular breaks are essential to maintaining energy. Use techniques like the Pomodoro Technique, or simply take a few minutes every hour to stand, stretch, and refresh. These pauses help prevent fatigue, restore focus, and reduce stress.
   - Incorporate longer breaks in the middle of the day to recharge. A short walk, a few deep breaths, or a healthy snack can make a significant difference in sustaining your energy for the afternoon.

4. **Fuel Your Body with Healthy Habits**:
   - Energy management is deeply connected to physical health. Stay hydrated, eat balanced meals, and avoid too much caffeine, which can lead to energy crashes. Prioritize foods rich in protein, healthy fats, and complex carbohydrates for steady energy throughout the day.
   - Movement is also essential: regular exercise, even light stretching or a brisk walk, can boost energy and improve focus.

5. **Incorporate Restorative Activities**:
   - Tasks that deplete your energy (such as focused work or extensive planning) should be balanced with activities that restore it. Incorporate a few minutes of mindfulness, breathing exercises, or meditation to recharge mentally and emotionally.

- o If possible, spend a few minutes outdoors each day. Natural light and fresh air are proven to improve mood, reduce stress, and boost energy.
6. **End Your Day with a Calming Routine**:
    - o As the day winds down, shift from high-energy tasks to more relaxed activities. A gentle evening routine helps your body transition to rest, promoting better sleep and giving your mind a chance to unwind.
    - o Avoid screens and intense activities before bed. Instead, engage in calming rituals, like reading, journaling, or light stretching, which prepare you for quality sleep—a critical factor in energy management.

Example of an Energy-Managed Day

Here's a sample structure of a day built around energy management principles:

1. **Morning (Peak Energy)**:
    - o Focus on high-impact tasks like project work, creative tasks, or decision-making.
    - o Use uninterrupted blocks of time for deep work, saving meetings or calls for later if possible.
2. **Mid-Morning Break**:
    - o Take a 5-10 minute break to stretch, move, or drink water. Use this time to reset and prevent fatigue.
3. **Late Morning (High Energy)**:
    - o Continue with priority tasks or start any medium-level tasks that require focus but aren't as demanding.
4. **Afternoon (Low Energy)**:
    - o Use this time for easier, routine tasks like email responses, scheduling, or administrative work.
    - o Consider a 15–30-minute break to recharge with a walk, snack, or short meditation.
5. **Late Afternoon (Moderate Energy)**:
    - o Wrap up the day with any remaining tasks that require focus but are manageable with moderate energy.
6. **Evening**:

—

- Transition to restorative activities. Focus on relaxing, connecting with loved ones, and engaging in light, enjoyable activities.

By structuring your day around your energy levels, you're able to approach each task with the focus, creativity, and patience it requires.

Reflection Exercise

In your journal, take a few minutes to reflect on these questions:

- **What are my natural energy peaks and valleys throughout the day?**
- **Which tasks would benefit most from my high-energy periods?**
- **How can I incorporate more energy-restorative activities into my day?**

Affirmations for Energy Management

To support your journey toward balanced energy, try these affirmations:

- "I honor my energy by working in harmony with my natural rhythms."
- "I am productive and focused when I align my tasks with my energy levels."
- "Rest and renewal are essential parts of my day, allowing me to thrive."

Moving Forward with Energy Management

Mastering energy management allows you to use your time more effectively, but with less stress and effort. By tuning into your natural rhythms, you're creating a sustainable approach to productivity that values well-being and balance. Embrace each day as a chance to listen to your body, prioritize meaningful work, and take breaks that truly recharge you.

As you continue to build this habit, you'll find that you can accomplish more with greater ease, making your work and personal life more fulfilling. Use today to start small, observing your energy patterns and choosing tasks that align with them, and let this be the beginning of a more intentional, energized journey toward your goals.

Day 21: Reflecting on Week 3 – Assessing Growth and Recalibrating Goals

Congratulations on completing Week 3! This week, you focused on productivity techniques like deep work, energy management, and overcoming procrastination. Today is a chance to pause, reflect on your journey, celebrate your progress, and recalibrate your goals as needed. Reflection is a powerful tool that allows you to recognize growth, learn from challenges, and make any adjustments that align with your evolving priorities.

In a journey toward personal and professional growth, reflection keeps you grounded. By taking a moment to look back on your experiences, you gain valuable insights, deepen your self-awareness, and affirm your commitment to continuous improvement. As you assess this week's progress, embrace each win, no matter how small, and use any setbacks as opportunities for growth.

The Importance of Reflection in Goal Achievement

Reflection creates space to celebrate progress, learn from obstacles, and reconnect with your intentions. Without regular reflection, it's easy to lose sight of your goals or feel overwhelmed by setbacks. Taking time to pause allows you to stay on track with a sense of purpose and flexibility. It's a reminder that growth is a journey, not a destination, and each experience—positive or challenging— contributes to your development.

This week's focus on time management, energy, and overcoming procrastination has likely given you insights into your habits, strengths, and areas for improvement. Use this reflection to gain clarity on what's working, what needs adjusting, and how to move forward with confidence.

Reflecting on Your Growth This Week

Use the following prompts to guide your reflection. Take a few minutes to answer each one honestly and thoughtfully in your journal:

1. **What Are My Accomplishments This Week?**
   o Celebrate every achievement, no matter the size. Did you complete more Pomodoro sessions than usual? Successfully manage your energy throughout the

day? Make note of these wins—they're a testament to your hard work and commitment.

2. **What Challenges Did I Encounter, and How Did I Respond?**
   - Reflect on any obstacles you faced, such as difficulty focusing, procrastination, or energy slumps. How did you handle these challenges? Acknowledge your efforts and think about what you could try differently if similar obstacles arise in the future.

3. **How Has My Approach to Productivity Shifted?**
   - Consider how the techniques you practiced—like energy management and deep work—impacted your approach to tasks. Do you feel more focused, energized, or in control of your time? Reflect on any positive shifts in mindset or habits that have emerged.

4. **What Have I Learned About My Energy Patterns and Work Preferences?**
   - Reflect on the insights you gained about your natural energy levels and when you're most productive. How can you continue to honor these patterns moving forward?

5. **What Areas Could Benefit from Recalibration?**
   - Consider if there's any area where your goals need adjusting. Perhaps a goal feels too ambitious and would benefit from smaller steps, or maybe you need to allocate more time for rest. Use these insights to make thoughtful adjustments that align with your needs and values.

Recalibrating Your Goals for the Coming Week

As you look ahead, think about any adjustments you'd like to make based on your reflections. Recalibration isn't about lowering expectations; it's about aligning your goals with your current reality and priorities. Here's how to recalibrate effectively:

1. **Reassess Your Top Priorities**:
   - Based on this week's insights, re-evaluate your top priorities. Are there tasks or goals that have become more or less important? Shift your focus accordingly,

—

83

ensuring your energy goes to what matters most right now.

2. **Adjust Time and Energy Commitments**:
   o   If you found certain goals or tasks too demanding, consider breaking them down into smaller, more manageable steps. Likewise, if you noticed an energy slump at certain times, schedule demanding tasks during peak energy periods to make the most of your natural rhythm.

3. **Set Specific, Achievable Goals for the Week**:
   o   Write down 2–3 specific goals for the coming week, making them realistic and actionable. For example, instead of "improve productivity," try "complete three Pomodoro sessions each morning" or "allocate two hours of focused work to a key project."

4. **Reinforce Self-Care and Rest**:
   o   Growth requires balance. Reflect on how you can incorporate self-care into your week, whether through rest, hobbies, or moments of mindfulness. Recharging is essential for sustainable progress.

Example of Recalibrating Goals

Let's say one of your original goals was to write 1,000 words each day. After reflecting, you realize that this goal felt overwhelming on certain days and impacted your energy for other tasks. Here's how you might recalibrate:

1. **Adjust the Goal**: Shift to writing 500 words each day or aim for three focused 25-minute writing sessions.
2. **Time Adjustment**: Schedule your writing during high-energy periods, such as the morning.
3. **Self-Care Addition**: Plan for a short walk or stretch after each writing session to recharge and maintain focus for the rest of the day.

This recalibration keeps the goal achievable and helps you maintain a sense of progress without feeling drained.

Reflection Exercise

In your journal, answer the following questions to wrap up your reflection and create a focused plan for the next week:

—

- **How have my actions this week brought me closer to my goals?**
- **What changes can I make to align my schedule and energy with my priorities?**
- **What small steps can I commit to in the coming week to keep momentum?**

Affirmations for Continued Growth and Adaptability

Use these affirmations to keep your mindset focused on growth, flexibility, and progress:

- "I celebrate each step forward, knowing that progress is a journey."
- "I adapt my goals to align with my needs, honoring my growth and well-being."
- "I am committed to my goals, and I adjust with confidence and resilience."

Moving Forward with Clarity and Confidence

Reflecting on your growth and recalibrating goals is a powerful way to stay connected to your journey. By honoring both your achievements and your challenges, you're creating a balanced approach to growth that values progress and self-awareness. Each recalibration brings you closer to achieving your goals in a way that aligns with your unique energy, preferences, and values.

As you continue this journey, let each reflection be a reminder of how far you've come and a stepping stone to where you're headed. Embrace each week as a chance to learn, grow, and recalibrate with purpose.

Week 4: Mindfulness and Inner Peace

Day 22: Introduction to Mindfulness – Being Present in the Moment

Today, we're introducing the practice of **mindfulness**—a simple yet transformative way of cultivating awareness, peace, and presence in daily life. Mindfulness is the art of being fully present, of bringing your attention to the here and now without judgment or distraction. In our fast-paced world, we're often caught up in worries about the future or replaying moments from the past. Mindfulness invites us to pause, observe, and truly experience each moment as it unfolds, creating space for clarity, calm, and self-connection.

Practicing mindfulness doesn't require hours of meditation or silence. It's an approach to life that can be incorporated into everyday tasks, from eating and walking to interacting with others. By learning to be more mindful, you're building a foundation of self-awareness, reducing stress, and nurturing a more balanced, fulfilling life.

Why Mindfulness Matters

Mindfulness is a powerful tool for managing stress, improving focus, and enhancing emotional well-being. Studies show that mindfulness can increase mental resilience, reduce symptoms of anxiety and depression, and even improve physical health. By anchoring yourself in the present, you're training your mind to engage fully in whatever you're doing, helping you build a stronger connection to yourself and the world around you.

When you're mindful, you're able to respond to situations with greater patience and clarity, rather than reacting impulsively. This shift brings more joy to simple moments, creating a sense of peace that is not dependent on external circumstances.

Getting Started with Mindfulness

Mindfulness is accessible to everyone, and you can start with just a few minutes each day. Here are some steps to help you begin your mindfulness journey:

1. **Start with the Breath**:
   o The breath is a natural anchor that brings you back to the present moment. Take a few deep breaths, paying close attention to each inhale and exhale. Notice the sensation of the air moving in and out of your body.
   o Whenever you find your mind wandering, gently bring your focus back to your breath. This simple practice of noticing your breathing helps create a sense of calm and focus.

2. **Observe Without Judgment**:
   o Mindfulness involves observing your thoughts, emotions, and physical sensations without judgment. As you practice, allow yourself to notice what's happening without labeling it as "good" or "bad."
   o For example, if you feel stressed, simply acknowledge the sensation without trying to change it. This nonjudgmental awareness helps reduce stress and creates space for acceptance.

3. **Use Your Senses to Ground Yourself**:
   o Engage your senses to fully experience the present moment. Notice what you can see, hear, feel, taste, and smell. This practice can be done anywhere, whether you're savoring a meal, walking in nature, or even washing dishes.
   o By focusing on sensory details, you shift your mind away from distractions and become more grounded in what's happening right now.

4. **Practice a Few Minutes of Mindful Meditation Daily**:
   o Set aside 5–10 minutes each day for a simple mindfulness meditation. Sit comfortably, close your eyes if you like, and bring your attention to your breath. Notice each inhale and exhale, allowing yourself to simply be present.

- o If thoughts arise, acknowledge them without judgment and gently return to your breath. This daily practice helps build a foundation of mindfulness, making it easier to bring presence into other areas of life.

5. **Bring Mindfulness to Everyday Activities**:
   - o Mindfulness isn't limited to meditation—it can be integrated into daily routines. Try practicing mindfulness while eating, walking, or even during conversations. Slow down, pay attention, and be fully engaged in whatever you're doing.
   - o For example, when eating, notice the colors, textures, and flavors of your food. This practice enhances enjoyment and keeps you connected to the present moment.

A Simple Mindfulness Exercise

Here's a quick mindfulness exercise you can try anytime to bring yourself back to the present:

1. **Take a Deep Breath**: Breathe in slowly and deeply, then exhale fully.
2. **Notice Your Body**: Bring your attention to your body, noticing any areas of tension or relaxation.
3. **Observe Your Surroundings**: Look around and identify five things you can see, four things you can feel, three things you can hear, two things you can smell, and one thing you can taste. This grounding exercise uses your senses to anchor you in the moment.

This practice takes just a few minutes and is especially helpful if you're feeling overwhelmed or distracted.

Benefits of Mindfulness

The practice of mindfulness brings numerous benefits to both mental and physical well-being. Here are just a few:

- **Reduced Stress**: Mindfulness helps calm the nervous system, lowering stress and promoting relaxation.
- **Improved Focus**: By training your mind to stay present, you increase your ability to concentrate on tasks.

- **Enhanced Emotional Awareness**: Mindfulness allows you to observe emotions without reacting impulsively, creating space for thoughtful responses.
- **Greater Joy and Gratitude**: When you're fully present, you experience life more vividly, noticing small moments of joy that might otherwise go unnoticed.

Reflection Exercise

In your journal, take a few moments to answer these questions to deepen your understanding of mindfulness and its role in your life:

- **When do I feel most present and aware of the moment?**
- **What distractions or thoughts often pull me away from the present?**
- **How can I incorporate more mindfulness into my daily routine?**

Affirmations for Cultivating Mindfulness

Use these affirmations to support your mindfulness practice and strengthen your commitment to being present:

- "I choose to be fully present in each moment, embracing life as it is."
- "My mind is calm, my heart is open, and I find peace in the here and now."
- "I release the past and future, finding joy in this moment."

Moving Forward with Mindfulness

Mindfulness is a journey, one that deepens with practice and patience. Each time you bring awareness to the present, you're taking a step toward greater peace, resilience, and connection. Remember, mindfulness doesn't require perfection—it's a practice of noticing, accepting, and coming back to the here and now, no matter how many times your mind may wander.

As you continue to explore mindfulness, give yourself permission to move at your own pace. Enjoy the small moments of presence, and trust that each mindful breath brings you closer to a life filled with clarity, calm, and fulfillment. Embrace mindfulness as a way of being, a gentle invitation to live fully and appreciate the beauty of each moment.

Day 23: Practicing Breathing Exercises for Calm and Focus

Today's focus is on **breathing exercises**—a simple but powerful way to create calm, focus, and mental clarity. Our breath is a natural anchor, always available to us, and by learning to control it, we can influence our nervous system, regulate stress, and shift our mind into a state of relaxation or alertness, depending on our needs. Breathing exercises are an accessible tool that can be practiced anytime, anywhere, making them ideal for finding calm and focus in any situation.

In our fast-paced lives, we often take shallow breaths, a habit that can increase tension and anxiety. Breathing exercises help you connect with deeper, slower breathing, which signals to your brain that it's safe to relax. Practicing these exercises regularly also enhances your awareness, helping you stay grounded and centered, even amid challenges.

Why Breathing Exercises Matter

Breathing exercises are beneficial for both mental and physical well-being. Studies show that deep, controlled breathing reduces stress hormones, lowers blood pressure, and promotes relaxation. When we're stressed, our body's "fight-or-flight" response often kicks in, making our breathing shallow and rapid. By practicing breathing exercises, we can activate the body's "rest-and-digest" response, which calms the nervous system and brings our mind back to a state of balance.

Focusing on the breath also trains the mind to stay present, making it an excellent tool for increasing mindfulness. Whether you're preparing for a big presentation, feeling overwhelmed, or just need a moment of calm, breathing exercises can help you reset.

Simple Breathing Techniques for Calm and Focus

Here are some effective breathing exercises to help you cultivate calm and focus. These techniques require no equipment and only a few minutes, making them easy to incorporate into your day.

1. Diaphragmatic Breathing (Belly Breathing)

This technique encourages deep breathing from the diaphragm, rather than shallow breaths from the chest. Diaphragmatic breathing helps reduce stress, increase oxygen intake, and improve focus.

How to Practice:
1. Sit or lie down in a comfortable position, placing one hand on your chest and the other on your belly.
2. Inhale slowly through your nose, allowing your belly to rise while keeping your chest still.
3. Exhale slowly through your mouth, feeling your belly fall as you release the air.
4. Repeat for 5–10 breaths, focusing on the rise and fall of your belly.

Benefits: Diaphragmatic breathing promotes relaxation, slows the heart rate, and helps anchor your mind in the present.

2. 4-7-8 Breathing

The 4-7-8 technique is a calming breath exercise often used for relaxation and stress reduction. It's especially helpful before bedtime, as it encourages a slow, steady breathing rhythm that signals your body to unwind.

How to Practice:
1. Inhale quietly through your nose for a count of 4.
2. Hold your breath for a count of 7.
3. Exhale completely through your mouth for a count of 8, making a whooshing sound.
4. Repeat for 4 cycles, and gradually increase to 8 cycles as you become comfortable.

Benefits: This exercise helps calm the nervous system, releases tension, and promotes a sense of tranquility.

3. Box Breathing (Square Breathing)

Box breathing is a structured exercise that creates balance and focus. It's often used by athletes, public speakers, and military personnel to increase concentration and calm before high-stress situations.

How to Practice:
1. Inhale through your nose for a count of 4.
2. Hold your breath for a count of 4.

3. Exhale slowly through your mouth for a count of 4.
4. Pause and hold your breath again for a count of 4.
5. Repeat for 4–5 cycles, keeping your breath smooth and steady.

Benefits: Box breathing stabilizes the breath, reduces anxiety, and enhances focus, making it ideal for moments when you need clarity and composure.

4. Alternate Nostril Breathing (Nadi Shodhana)

This ancient yoga breathing technique balances the left and right hemispheres of the brain, promoting a sense of calm and mental clarity. It's ideal for times when you need to feel centered and focused.

How to Practice:
1. Sit comfortably and hold your right thumb over your right nostril, gently closing it.
2. Inhale slowly through your left nostril.
3. Close your left nostril with your right ring finger, then open your right nostril and exhale through it.
4. Inhale through the right nostril, then close it with your thumb, open the left nostril, and exhale through it.
5. Continue alternating nostrils for 5–10 cycles.

Benefits: Alternate nostril breathing calms the mind, reduces stress, and enhances concentration, bringing a balanced sense of energy.

Creating a Breathing Practice Routine

To experience the full benefits of breathing exercises, consider incorporating them into your daily routine. Here's a simple plan to get started:
1. **Morning**: Begin your day with a few minutes of diaphragmatic breathing to set a calm and focused tone for the day.
2. **Midday Break**: Use box breathing during breaks to recharge your mind and reduce stress.
3. **Evening**: Practice 4-7-8 breathing before bed to help your body relax and prepare for restful sleep.

Over time, you'll find that these exercises become a natural tool you can use whenever you need to reduce stress, increase focus, or simply feel more grounded.

———

Reflection Exercise

In your journal, take a few moments to answer these questions and reflect on your experience with breathing exercises:

- **How did I feel before and after practicing breathing exercises?**
- **Which technique resonated with me the most, and why?**
- **How can I incorporate breathing exercises into moments of stress or distraction?**

Affirmations for Calm and Focus

To support your breathing practice, try using these affirmations to reinforce calm and focus:

- "I breathe in peace, and I breathe out tension."
- "With each breath, I become more centered and focused."
- "My breath grounds me in the present, bringing calm and clarity."

Moving Forward with Mindful Breathing

Breathing exercises are a simple but profound way to nurture calm and focus in your daily life. By practicing these techniques, you're learning to listen to your body's natural rhythms, reconnect with the present moment, and find peace within yourself. Each breath you take with intention is a step toward greater balance, resilience, and clarity.

Embrace mindful breathing as a valuable tool for self-care and grounding, one you can turn to whenever you need a moment of calm or a boost in focus. Let your breath be a source of strength and serenity, guiding you through life's challenges and bringing you back to the simplicity and peace of the present moment.

Day 24: Managing Stress – Letting Go of Control

Today's focus is on a powerful way to manage stress: **letting go of control**. Often, stress arises when we try to control everything around us—situations, outcomes, other people's reactions—only to find that most things in life are beyond our control. Learning to let go of this need for control can be liberating, reducing stress and creating a sense of peace. By accepting that some things are simply outside of our influence, we open ourselves to living with greater flexibility, resilience, and calm.

Letting go of control doesn't mean being passive; it's about choosing to release the worry and tension that comes from trying to manage every detail. When you focus on what you can control—your thoughts, actions, and responses—you free yourself from the weight of unrealistic expectations and start approaching challenges with a calm, grounded mindset.

Why Letting Go of Control Reduces Stress

Our desire to control is often rooted in fear: fear of uncertainty, fear of failure, fear of not being enough. By trying to control outcomes, we seek to eliminate these fears, but this approach only increases stress and tension. When we accept that some things are beyond our control, we can let go of this inner struggle, allowing us to approach life's challenges with a more open mind and heart.

Research shows that accepting things we can't control can lead to increased mental well-being, reduced anxiety, and greater resilience. Letting go shifts our focus from what's out of reach to what's within our power, creating a sense of clarity, empowerment, and inner peace.

Steps to Let Go of Control and Manage Stress

Learning to let go of control is a process that takes self-awareness and patience. Here's a guide to help you start releasing the need for control and manage stress with greater ease:

1. **Identify What's Within Your Control**:
    o   Reflect on a stressful situation and identify what aspects of it you can influence and what aspects you cannot. For example, you can control your response to a challenge but not the actions of others.

- Make a list of what is within your control (such as your thoughts, choices, and responses) and what is outside of your control (like external circumstances or other people's opinions). This clarity helps you focus your energy on what you can change.

2. **Practice Acceptance**:
   - Acceptance doesn't mean liking or agreeing with a situation; it simply means acknowledging reality as it is. When you find yourself trying to control something you can't, take a moment to accept it without resistance.
   - Practice saying to yourself, "This is how things are right now," and allow yourself to feel whatever emotions arise. Acceptance helps you move from resistance to peace, easing the inner tension that control often creates.

3. **Shift Your Focus to the Present Moment**:
   - Stress often arises from worrying about future outcomes or ruminating on the past. When you bring your attention to the present, you're focusing on the only moment you truly have control over.
   - Use mindfulness practices, like deep breathing or grounding exercises, to bring yourself back to the here and now. Embracing the present moment reduces the urge to control and helps you feel more connected to what's happening right now.

4. **Challenge Perfectionism**:
   - Perfectionism is closely linked to the need for control, as it stems from the belief that we must get everything "just right." Recognize that imperfection is a natural part of life and growth.
   - Remind yourself that it's okay to make mistakes and that flexibility is a sign of strength. By letting go of perfectionism, you're creating space for learning, spontaneity, and joy.

5. **Embrace Flexibility and Adaptability**:

- o Life is full of unexpected changes, and learning to adapt helps reduce stress. Embrace flexibility by allowing room for change in your plans or expectations.
  - o Approach challenges with a mindset of curiosity, asking, "How can I work with this?" rather than "How can I make this go exactly as planned?" This perspective shift helps you respond to changes with resilience rather than stress.

6. **Use Letting Go Affirmations**:
   - o Affirmations can help reinforce your commitment to releasing control and finding peace. Phrases like, "I release what I cannot control," or "I am open to the flow of life" serve as gentle reminders to let go and trust the process.

Practicing Letting Go Through Breathing Exercises

Breathing exercises are a great way to reinforce the practice of letting go. Here's a simple exercise to help you release tension and find a sense of calm:

1. **Inhale Deeply**: Take a deep breath, imagining you're breathing in acceptance and peace.
2. **Exhale Slowly**: As you exhale, imagine releasing stress and the need for control.
3. **Repeat with Intention**: Continue this breathing pattern for several breaths, repeating the affirmation, "With each exhale, I release what I cannot control."

This exercise helps shift your focus from control to calm, grounding you in the present moment and bringing a sense of release.

Reflection Exercise

In your journal, take a few moments to answer these questions to deepen your understanding of letting go and its impact on stress:

- **What areas of my life do I try to control most? Why?**
- **How would I feel if I released the need to control this area?**
- **What can I focus on instead, that is within my control?**

Affirmations for Letting Go and Reducing Stress

Use these affirmations to support your journey of letting go and creating inner peace:

- "I release the need to control outcomes; I trust in my ability to handle whatever comes."
- "I am at peace with what I cannot change, and I focus on what I can."
- "Each day, I find strength in letting go and embracing life as it is."

Moving Forward with Acceptance and Calm

Letting go of control is a journey, one that requires patience, practice, and self-compassion. As you learn to release what you cannot change, you're freeing yourself from the stress and tension that control brings. This act of surrender doesn't mean giving up; it means finding the wisdom and strength to focus on what truly matters—your thoughts, choices, and presence in each moment.

Embrace the process of letting go as a pathway to peace, resilience, and freedom. Each time you release the need to control, you're creating space for calm, clarity, and a greater connection to yourself and the world around you. Let today be a reminder that true strength comes not from controlling everything, but from trusting yourself to handle whatever comes, with grace and an open heart.

Day 25: Embracing Minimalism – Prioritizing What Matters

Today's focus is on the concept of **minimalism**—a lifestyle approach that encourages you to let go of excess and focus on what truly matters. Minimalism isn't just about having fewer possessions; it's about creating a life filled with purpose, clarity, and intention. By consciously choosing to focus on what adds value, minimalism helps you clear both physical and mental clutter, allowing you to dedicate your energy to the people, activities, and goals that bring you the most fulfillment.

In a world that often celebrates more, minimalism is a refreshing approach to finding joy in simplicity. It's a way to declutter your life, let go of what doesn't serve you, and make room for the things that genuinely matter. Embracing minimalism invites you to prioritize your time, resources, and attention with a sense of purpose, creating a life that reflects your true values and aspirations.

Why Embracing Minimalism Matters

Minimalism isn't about restriction; it's about liberation. When we clear away the physical and emotional excess, we gain the freedom to focus on what enriches our lives. Research shows that reducing clutter can lead to lower stress, greater focus, and improved mental health. By simplifying your environment, responsibilities, and even your goals, you're giving yourself the space to grow and the freedom to live with intention.

Minimalism helps you realign with your values, giving you more time and energy to invest in meaningful relationships, personal growth, and creative pursuits. It's a reminder that sometimes, less truly is more.

Steps to Embrace Minimalism and Prioritize What Matters

Embracing minimalism is a gradual journey that involves both reflection and action. Here's a guide to help you get started on simplifying your life and focusing on what's truly important:

1. **Define Your Core Values and Priorities**:

- Start by reflecting on what matters most to you. What brings you joy? What aligns with your long-term goals? Write down your core values and top priorities. These will serve as your guiding compass for deciding what to keep and what to let go.
- Having a clear sense of purpose makes it easier to release what doesn't align with your values, whether it's physical items, time commitments, or mental clutter.

2. **Declutter Your Physical Space**:
   - Begin with a small area, like your desk, closet, or a drawer. Go through each item, asking yourself if it adds value to your life. If it doesn't serve a purpose or bring you joy, consider letting it go.
   - Physical clutter can create mental stress, so by clearing your environment, you're creating a space that promotes focus, relaxation, and peace.

3. **Simplify Your Schedule**:
   - Look at your daily and weekly commitments. Are there activities or responsibilities that don't align with your priorities? Consider scaling back on obligations that don't add value to your life.
   - Minimalism in time management means choosing quality over quantity, giving yourself space to rest, reflect, and invest energy where it matters most.

4. **Practice Mindful Consumption**:
   - Minimalism isn't just about letting go; it's also about being intentional with what you bring into your life. Practice mindful consumption by asking yourself if a new purchase, relationship, or commitment aligns with your values.
   - By choosing quality over quantity, you can avoid unnecessary purchases or activities, leading to a more fulfilling and purpose-driven life.

5. **Let Go of Mental Clutter**:

- o Minimalism isn't limited to physical items—it also includes clearing your mind of unnecessary thoughts, worries, or distractions. Practice mindfulness, journaling, or meditation to release mental clutter and focus on what truly matters.
- o Letting go of unproductive thoughts creates mental space, helping you approach each day with clarity and calm.

6. **Nurture Meaningful Relationships**:
- o Minimalism also applies to relationships. Focus on nurturing connections with people who align with your values, support your growth, and bring positivity to your life. Limit time spent on relationships that drain your energy or don't serve your well-being.
- o Quality relationships are a key aspect of a minimalist life, providing joy and support without adding unnecessary stress or complexity.

A Minimalist Approach to Goal-Setting

Applying minimalism to your goals helps you focus on what's truly important, reducing the stress of endless to-do lists. Here's how to simplify your approach to goal-setting:

- **Choose 1–3 Priority Goals**: Instead of spreading yourself thin, select a few meaningful goals that align with your core values. These goals should be specific and achievable, allowing you to focus your energy on what brings the most satisfaction.
- **Set Clear, Intentional Actions**: For each goal, outline simple, actionable steps that move you toward completion. Minimalist goals focus on purposeful actions rather than exhaustive lists, helping you make steady progress without overwhelm.
- **Celebrate Small Wins**: Minimalism emphasizes presence and gratitude. Celebrate each step forward, recognizing that every small achievement contributes to a life of purpose and fulfillment.

Reflection Exercise

In your journal, answer the following questions to explore how minimalism can enhance your life and help you prioritize what matters:

- **What are my top three values, and how can I align my life more closely with them?**
- **What items or commitments can I let go of to create more space for joy and purpose?**
- **How can I simplify my daily routine to focus on what truly matters?**

Affirmations for Embracing Minimalism

Use these affirmations to support your journey toward a simpler, more intentional life:

- "I release what doesn't serve me, making space for what truly matters."
- "I choose quality over quantity, focusing on what brings me joy and fulfillment."
- "My life is filled with purpose, clarity, and simplicity."

Moving Forward with a Minimalist Mindset

Embracing minimalism is an empowering choice that invites you to live with intention, clarity, and freedom. Each time you let go of what doesn't align with your values, you're creating a life that reflects who you truly are. Minimalism isn't about perfection; it's about being mindful of what you keep and how you spend your time and energy. As you continue your journey, let each step toward simplicity remind you that true fulfillment comes from quality, not quantity. By focusing on what matters most, you're building a life filled with purpose, joy, and inner peace. Embrace minimalism as a way to live deeply, savor each moment, and create a space where your truest self can thrive.

Day 26: Gratitude and Perspective – Finding Joy in Simple Things

Today's focus is on **gratitude** and **perspective**—two practices that bring joy and meaning to life by shifting our focus to the abundance that surrounds us. When we embrace gratitude, we learn to see life through a lens of appreciation, savoring small moments that might otherwise go unnoticed. By practicing gratitude and gaining a fresh perspective, we can cultivate a deep sense of contentment and joy, even in the simplest of things.

Gratitude is more than an emotion; it's a habit that, when practiced regularly, rewires the brain to seek and recognize positive moments. Research shows that gratitude can improve well-being, increase resilience, and lower stress levels. By choosing gratitude, you're training your mind to focus on what you have rather than what you lack, fostering a spirit of thankfulness and joy.

Why Finding Joy in Simple Things Matters

In our busy lives, it's easy to become focused on big achievements or future goals, waiting for these moments to bring us happiness. But true joy is often found in the present, in small, everyday moments—the warmth of the sun, a kind word, or the taste of a favorite meal. When we slow down to appreciate these simple things, we connect more deeply with life's richness and beauty.

Practicing gratitude for life's simple pleasures brings a sense of peace and presence. It reminds us that happiness doesn't always come from grand experiences or possessions, but from noticing and appreciating what's around us right now.

How to Cultivate Gratitude and Perspective

Developing a gratitude practice is a simple yet powerful way to shift your perspective and find joy in everyday life. Here are steps to help you start recognizing and savoring the small moments:

1. **Keep a Gratitude Journal**:
    o Each day, write down three things you're grateful for. These can be big or small, from a loving conversation to the feeling of your morning coffee. Reflect on why each one brings you joy.

- Consistently journaling about gratitude trains your mind to look for positive moments, creating a habit of appreciation.

2. **Notice Small Moments Throughout the Day**:
   - Throughout your day, take small pauses to notice and appreciate what's happening around you. Feel the warmth of the sun, listen to the laughter of loved ones, or savor the smell of a favorite meal.
   - These small pauses allow you to experience the richness of each moment, creating a deeper connection to life.

3. **Shift Your Perspective During Challenges**:
   - When you face challenges, look for silver linings or lessons within them. Ask yourself, "What can I learn from this?" or "What positive outcome might come from this experience?"
   - While it's natural to feel frustration or sadness during difficulties, practicing gratitude for the growth they bring can ease stress and build resilience.

4. **Express Appreciation to Others**:
   - Take time to show gratitude for the people in your life. Send a note, make a call, or simply tell someone you appreciate them. Expressing gratitude not only strengthens your relationships but also enhances your own sense of happiness.
   - Genuine expressions of appreciation bring warmth to both you and those around you, reinforcing connections and spreading positivity.

5. **Reframe Negative Thoughts with Gratitude**:
   - When you find yourself focusing on what's missing or feeling dissatisfied, try to reframe your thoughts with gratitude. Instead of thinking, "I wish I had more time," try, "I'm grateful for the time I had today to focus on what matters."
   - This practice shifts your mindset from scarcity to abundance, helping you find peace in the present.

6. **Reflect on Simple Joys at the End of Each Day**:

- Before bed, reflect on a few moments of joy from your day. These don't have to be big events; they could be as simple as a smile from a stranger or a delicious meal. Embracing these moments of joy strengthens your sense of gratitude.
- This nightly reflection helps reinforce the habit of seeing and appreciating life's everyday blessings.

A Simple Gratitude Exercise

Here's a short exercise you can do to connect with gratitude and perspective:

1. **Pause and Take a Deep Breath**: Close your eyes, take a deep breath, and center yourself.
2. **Think of One Simple Joy from Today**: Bring to mind a small, joyful moment you experienced today—a gentle breeze, a moment of laughter, or a kind interaction.
3. **Reflect on Why It Matters**: Take a moment to reflect on why this small joy brings you happiness and what it adds to your life.
4. **Express Silent Thanks**: Silently express gratitude for this moment, acknowledging it as a gift and a source of joy.

This exercise can be done anytime during the day when you need a moment of calm or a reminder of life's beauty.

Benefits of Practicing Gratitude

Gratitude offers many mental, emotional, and physical benefits, including:

- **Improved Mood**: Gratitude boosts happiness and reduces symptoms of anxiety and depression by shifting focus to positive aspects of life.
- **Enhanced Resilience**: By recognizing the good, gratitude helps build resilience, allowing you to handle stress and challenges more gracefully.
- **Stronger Relationships**: Expressing gratitude deepens your relationships, fostering a sense of connection and mutual appreciation.

Reflection Exercise

In your journal, take a few minutes to reflect on the following prompts to deepen your gratitude practice:

- **What small things bring me joy every day that I often overlook?**
- **How can I create more moments of gratitude and appreciation in my daily life?**
- **Who in my life deserves my gratitude, and how can I express it to them?**

Affirmations for Gratitude and Joy

Use these affirmations to reinforce a grateful mindset and remind yourself to find joy in the simple things:

- "I find joy in the simple moments, appreciating life's everyday blessings."
- "Gratitude fills my heart, bringing peace and happiness to each day."
- "I am grateful for the abundance that surrounds me, both big and small."

Moving Forward with Gratitude and Perspective

Practicing gratitude is a choice that brings you closer to a life of fulfillment and peace. Each moment of appreciation strengthens your ability to find joy in the present and embrace life's gifts, no matter how small they may seem. As you continue your journey, let gratitude be a guiding light that shifts your perspective, helping you see beauty in the world around you and connect with the simple joys that make life rich.

Embrace each day as an opportunity to practice gratitude, knowing that this simple act can transform your experience of the world. Allow gratitude to open your heart, broaden your perspective, and fill your life with the joy of truly seeing and appreciating what is already here. In this way, you're creating a life filled with peace, abundance, and deep, lasting contentment.

Day 27: Releasing Negative Emotions Through Forgiveness

Today's focus is on **forgiveness**—a profound practice that allows you to release negative emotions and create space for peace, healing, and growth. Forgiveness doesn't mean forgetting or excusing harmful actions; rather, it's an act of letting go of the anger, resentment, and hurt that weigh on your heart. By forgiving, you're choosing to free yourself from the grip of painful emotions, making room for healing, compassion, and a deeper sense of inner peace.

Holding onto negative emotions can drain your energy and impact your mental and physical well-being. When we refuse to forgive, we keep the past alive in the present, replaying painful events and feelings over and over. Forgiveness is an intentional decision to stop carrying these burdens. By releasing resentment, you reclaim your power, taking control of your emotional health and giving yourself the freedom to move forward.

Why Forgiveness Matters for Inner Peace

Forgiveness is a gift you give yourself. Studies show that practicing forgiveness can reduce stress, lower blood pressure, improve mental health, and even boost immune function. The act of forgiving releases you from the toxic cycle of negative emotions, giving you the opportunity to experience greater compassion, joy, and resilience.

Forgiveness is also an act of self-respect, as it allows you to take control of your own healing and well-being. When you choose to forgive, you're not condoning what happened; you're choosing to prioritize your own peace and happiness over lingering anger or hurt.

Steps to Practice Forgiveness and Release Negative Emotions

Forgiveness is a journey that requires self-compassion and patience. Here's a step-by-step guide to help you begin this powerful process of letting go:

1. **Acknowledge Your Feelings**:
   o Start by recognizing and accepting the emotions you're holding onto. Whether it's anger, hurt, disappointment, or betrayal, allow yourself to fully feel these emotions without judgment. This honest acknowledgment is the first step toward healing.

- Write down what you're feeling, describing the situation and its impact on you. This helps bring clarity to your emotions and validates your experience.

2. **Reflect on the Situation with Compassion**:
   - Try to understand the other person's perspective, even if you don't agree with their actions. Ask yourself, "What might have motivated their behavior?" or "What pain or limitation might they have been experiencing?" Cultivating compassion doesn't mean excusing their actions, but it can help you understand that everyone carries their own struggles.
   - Remember that compassion includes yourself. Be gentle with yourself, acknowledging that your feelings are valid and that forgiveness is a gradual process.

3. **Set an Intention to Forgive**:
   - Forgiveness starts with a conscious choice. Set an intention to forgive, even if you're not yet sure how to fully let go. Repeat to yourself, "I am choosing to forgive for my own peace," or "I release this burden for my healing."
   - This intention plants the seed of forgiveness, allowing your heart to open over time, even if the process feels challenging at first.

4. **Practice Letting Go Through Visualization**:
   - Close your eyes and imagine holding onto the pain or resentment as if it's a physical object. Visualize yourself gently releasing it, watching it dissolve or drift away, leaving you feeling lighter and more at ease.
   - Visualization helps reinforce your intention to let go, creating a mental and emotional release that supports forgiveness.

5. **Release Negative Emotions with Affirmations**:

- Use affirmations to reinforce your decision to forgive and to replace negative emotions with peace and compassion. Try repeating, "I release anger and embrace peace," or "I choose forgiveness and open my heart to healing."
- Affirmations help reframe your mindset, allowing forgiveness to become a source of strength and freedom.

6. **Find Gratitude and Lessons in the Experience**:
   - Reflect on any lessons the experience taught you. Perhaps it made you stronger, more resilient, or more compassionate. Embracing the growth that came from a difficult situation can help bring closure.
   - Practice gratitude by acknowledging how this experience, even with its challenges, has contributed to your personal growth. Gratitude shifts your focus from pain to growth, allowing forgiveness to flow more easily.

Practicing Forgiveness for Yourself

Forgiveness isn't only about releasing others; it's also about forgiving yourself. If you're holding onto guilt or regret for past mistakes, consider offering yourself the same compassion and understanding you'd offer a friend. Self-forgiveness is essential to healing, as it frees you from self-blame and allows you to move forward with self-love.

1. **Acknowledge Mistakes with Compassion**: Recognize that everyone makes mistakes, and that growth often comes from learning from them. Allow yourself to see these mistakes as part of your journey, not as a reflection of your worth.

2. **Set an Intention for Self-Forgiveness**: Say to yourself, "I forgive myself for my mistakes and allow myself to grow." Repeat this daily, letting self-forgiveness become a healing mantra.

3. **Celebrate Progress, Not Perfection**: Remember, the goal is growth, not perfection. Embrace your progress and give yourself permission to move forward with a sense of renewed peace and acceptance.

Reflection Exercise

In your journal, take a few moments to answer these questions to deepen your forgiveness practice and release negative emotions:

- **Who or what do I need to forgive to experience peace?**
- **What benefits will forgiveness bring to my life? How will I feel once I release these emotions?**
- **What lessons can I learn from this experience that contribute to my personal growth?**

Affirmations for Forgiveness and Emotional Freedom

Use these affirmations to support your journey of forgiveness and create space for inner peace:

- "I release resentment and welcome peace into my heart."
- "Forgiveness frees me from the past and allows me to live fully in the present."
- "I choose compassion, healing, and freedom for myself and others."

Moving Forward with Forgiveness and Peace

Forgiveness is a powerful, transformative act that allows you to reclaim your peace, freedom, and joy. As you continue this journey, remember that forgiveness is for you—it's a gift of release, a way to lighten your heart and mind. Each time you let go of negative emotions, you're making space for positive energy, growth, and new possibilities.

Embrace forgiveness as a lifelong practice, one that brings deeper compassion, wisdom, and inner peace. Letting go doesn't erase the past; it frees you from its grip, allowing you to live more fully and joyfully in the present. Moving forward, choose forgiveness as a tool for healing, growth, and self-love. With each act of forgiveness, you're building a life that reflects strength, compassion, and peace.

Day 28: Building Inner Peace with Guided Meditation

Today's focus is on **guided meditation**—a practice that helps you cultivate inner peace, calm, and connection by guiding your mind through relaxation and visualization. Meditation can be challenging when you're just starting, especially when your mind is filled with thoughts and distractions. Guided meditation offers a gentle path to mindfulness by providing structured guidance that helps focus your mind, making it easier to access a state of inner peace.

Guided meditation is a simple, effective way to step out of the busy flow of everyday life and reconnect with your sense of calm and well-being. Through soft prompts and soothing visualizations, you'll learn to let go of tension, release anxious thoughts, and embrace the present moment. Practicing meditation regularly not only reduces stress but also nurtures resilience, self-awareness, and a lasting sense of tranquility.

Why Guided Meditation Supports Inner Peace

Guided meditation helps quiet the mind by focusing on a specific intention, visualization, or relaxation technique. When you follow a gentle voice or audio guide, you're less likely to feel overwhelmed by thoughts, as your attention is directed toward soothing imagery or calming instructions. Studies show that meditation has numerous benefits, including reduced stress, improved mental clarity, and enhanced emotional well-being. By setting aside even just a few minutes each day for guided meditation, you're creating a habit that fosters balance, relaxation, and a stronger connection to inner peace. Meditation also allows you to observe your thoughts and emotions without judgment, helping you develop mindfulness and resilience. When practiced regularly, it becomes a tool for managing stress and finding calm amidst life's challenges.

Getting Started with Guided Meditation

If you're new to meditation, guided meditation is a great way to begin. Here's a simple approach to help you get started and integrate meditation into your routine:

1. **Choose a Comfortable, Quiet Space**:

o   Find a quiet, comfortable place where you can sit or lie down without distractions. This can be anywhere—your bedroom, a cozy corner, or even outside in nature.

o   Make sure you're relaxed and comfortable, as physical comfort is key to fully immersing yourself in the meditation.

2. **Select a Guided Meditation**:

o   Choose a guided meditation that resonates with your needs. There are meditations focused on relaxation, stress relief, self-love, and mindfulness. Many apps and websites offer free options, so explore and find one that suits you.

o   Beginners may start with a short meditation, around 5–10 minutes, gradually increasing the duration as you feel more comfortable.

3. **Set an Intention for Peace**:

o   Begin by setting a simple intention, such as "I am here to find peace," or "I release stress and welcome calm." Setting an intention helps focus your mind and provides a gentle reminder of your purpose.

o   This intention can be something you return to throughout the meditation, creating a sense of grounding and purpose.

4. **Follow the Guide's Voice and Instructions**:

o   Allow yourself to follow the guide's voice fully, relaxing into the instructions. Notice any areas of tension in your body and gently release them as you breathe.

o   As the guide takes you through visualizations or breath work, try to immerse yourself in each step, focusing on the sensations and images that arise.

5. **Observe and Release Your Thoughts**:

o   If thoughts come up, simply acknowledge them without judgment and return your attention to the guide. Don't worry about "clearing your mind"; instead, allow yourself to be present with the meditation, even if your mind wanders.

o Meditation is a practice, and letting go of control over your thoughts is part of the process. Be gentle with yourself and remember that inner peace comes from acceptance.

6. **End with Gratitude and Reflection**:
   o As the meditation concludes, take a moment to feel gratitude for the peace you've cultivated. Place a hand over your heart and thank yourself for setting aside this time for inner peace and self-care.
   o Reflect on how you feel—more relaxed, clear-minded, or simply more present—and carry this sense of calm with you as you return to your day.

Sample Guided Meditation Script for Inner Peace

Here is a brief guided meditation script you can use for creating a sense of peace and calm:

1. **Find Your Breath**: Close your eyes, take a deep breath in, and release it slowly. Feel the natural rhythm of your breath as it flows in and out, anchoring you to the present.

2. **Relax Your Body**: Start at the top of your head and slowly relax each part of your body. Let go of any tension in your forehead, your shoulders, your chest, and your legs. Allow your entire body to sink into relaxation.

3. **Visualize a Place of Peace**: Imagine yourself in a peaceful setting, perhaps a quiet forest, a tranquil beach, or a garden filled with flowers. See yourself surrounded by beauty, feeling calm, safe, and at ease.

4. **Breathe in Peace, Exhale Tension**: With each breath, imagine inhaling a sense of peace and calm, and exhaling any stress or tension. Feel your whole body becoming lighter, filled with a soft, gentle calm.

5. **Stay Present**: If thoughts arise, acknowledge them and gently let them float away like clouds. Bring your attention back to the feeling of peace within you, returning to the breath and the calm of your chosen peaceful place.

6. **End with Gratitude**: As you take a final deep breath, place a hand on your heart and express gratitude for this moment of inner peace. Thank yourself for showing up, for caring for your well-being, and carry this peace forward as you open your eyes.

Benefits of Guided Meditation

Guided meditation offers numerous benefits, including:

- **Reduced Stress and Anxiety**: Meditation activates the body's relaxation response, reducing stress and calming the mind.
- **Enhanced Emotional Awareness**: By observing your thoughts without judgment, meditation builds emotional awareness and resilience.
- **Improved Focus and Clarity**: Guided meditation can improve concentration, helping you feel clear-minded and more focused throughout your day.
- **Deeper Connection to Self**: Meditation fosters a connection to your inner self, helping you feel more grounded and at peace.

Reflection Exercise

In your journal, take a few minutes to reflect on the following prompts:

- **How did I feel before and after practicing guided meditation?**
- **What sensations or thoughts came up during the meditation?**
- **How can I integrate meditation into my daily routine to nurture inner peace?**

Affirmations for Peace and Clarity

To support your meditation practice, use these affirmations to reinforce inner peace:

- "I am at peace in this moment, calm and connected."
- "With each breath, I release stress and welcome tranquility."
- "I carry a deep sense of peace within me, no matter what arises."

Moving Forward with Meditation and Peace

Guided meditation is a gentle yet powerful practice for creating inner peace. Each time you meditate, you're taking a step toward a life filled with calm, clarity, and resilience. Remember, meditation is a practice—it's okay if your mind wanders or if some days feel easier than others. Embrace each session as an opportunity to reconnect with yourself and bring a sense of peace into your day.

As you continue to explore meditation, allow yourself to grow at your own pace. Let meditation be a source of comfort, a moment of stillness, and a way to come home to yourself. Carry this sense of peace forward, knowing that it's always within you, accessible with every breath, guiding you toward a life of greater balance, ease, and fulfillment.

Day 29: Letting Go of Perfectionism

Today's focus is on **letting go of perfectionism**—a habit that can hold you back from embracing your full potential and experiencing true joy. Perfectionism is the tendency to set impossibly high standards for yourself, often tied to the fear of making mistakes or being judged. While striving for excellence can be positive, perfectionism often leads to stress, self-doubt, and even procrastination as we try to avoid failure or falling short of unrealistic expectations.

Letting go of perfectionism isn't about lowering your standards or accepting mediocrity; it's about choosing progress over perfection and embracing growth, learning, and self-compassion. By releasing the need to be perfect, you open yourself to new possibilities, gain confidence, and experience a greater sense of freedom and satisfaction. Today, you'll explore ways to let go of perfectionism and embrace a mindset that values effort, growth, and self-acceptance.

Why Letting Go of Perfectionism Matters

Perfectionism can be mentally and emotionally exhausting, creating a constant need for approval and success that is rarely fulfilling. Studies show that perfectionism is linked to anxiety, depression, and a fear of failure, which can ultimately hinder productivity, creativity, and happiness. By letting go of perfectionism, you're allowing yourself to be human, to make mistakes, and to grow in a way that's authentic and sustainable.

Embracing imperfection allows you to approach life with flexibility, resilience, and compassion. It gives you permission to learn from experiences rather than judging yourself by rigid standards, creating a mindset that values growth over flawless outcomes.

Steps to Let Go of Perfectionism

Letting go of perfectionism is a journey that takes self-awareness and practice. Here are some steps to help you release perfectionistic habits and embrace a more balanced, fulfilling approach:

1. **Recognize the Signs of Perfectionism**:

- Start by noticing when perfectionism shows up in your life. Do you hesitate to start projects for fear of failure? Are you overly critical of yourself or others? Do you avoid challenges unless you're certain you'll succeed?
- By identifying these tendencies, you create awareness of how perfectionism influences your actions and emotions, making it easier to address.

2. **Set Realistic, Achievable Goals**:
   - Instead of setting unrealistically high standards, break down goals into smaller, achievable steps. This approach reduces overwhelm and allows you to celebrate progress along the way.
   - Remember, success doesn't come from doing everything perfectly—it comes from consistent effort and learning. Aim for goals that challenge you, but that don't require perfection.

3. **Shift Your Focus to Growth Over Outcomes**:
   - Perfectionism often ties self-worth to outcomes rather than the process. Focus on what you can learn from each experience, regardless of the result. Celebrate your growth, effort, and the resilience you show along the way.
   - By valuing progress over perfection, you shift your perspective from seeking flawless results to embracing the journey of self-improvement.

4. **Practice Self-Compassion**:
   - Perfectionism can be harsh, holding you to standards that you would likely never expect of others. Treat yourself with the same kindness you'd offer a friend. When you make a mistake or fall short, practice self-compassion by reminding yourself that no one is perfect and that growth often involves trial and error.
   - Self-compassion encourages resilience, helping you bounce back from setbacks with a sense of acceptance and self-respect.

5. **Redefine Success and Failure**:

- Reframe your understanding of success and failure. Recognize that both success and failure are part of the learning process, and that each experience provides valuable lessons. Instead of viewing failure as a flaw, see it as a stepping stone toward growth.
- Embrace the idea that doing your best is enough, and that perfection is neither possible nor necessary for meaningful achievement.

6. **Celebrate Small Wins**:
   - Perfectionism can make it easy to overlook achievements in favor of focusing on what could be better. Take time to acknowledge and celebrate each small success, no matter how minor it may seem. By recognizing progress, you reinforce a positive mindset and build confidence in your abilities.
   - These small celebrations remind you that effort and consistency are valuable in themselves, even if the outcome isn't perfect.

A Simple Exercise to Practice Letting Go of Perfectionism

Here's a quick exercise to help you reframe your mindset and release perfectionistic tendencies:

1. **Write Down a Recent Challenge**: Think of a situation where perfectionism affected you—perhaps a project, task, or personal goal.
2. **Identify the Expectations**: Write down the expectations you set for yourself. Were they realistic, or were they influenced by a need for perfection?
3. **Reframe the Experience with Growth in Mind**: Reflect on what you learned from the experience. What skills did you develop? How did the challenge contribute to your growth?
4. **Set a New, Compassionate Goal**: Based on what you learned, set a goal that values growth over perfection. For example, "I will focus on making consistent progress" rather than "I must get this exactly right."

This exercise helps you see challenges through a lens of growth and self-compassion, allowing you to let go of rigid expectations and celebrate your effort.

Benefits of Releasing Perfectionism

Letting go of perfectionism brings numerous mental and emotional benefits, including:

- **Increased Resilience**: When you release the need to be perfect, you're more adaptable and open to learning from mistakes, which enhances resilience.
- **Greater Joy and Satisfaction**: Embracing imperfection allows you to experience life with more joy, celebrating small wins and savoring each moment.
- **Reduced Stress and Anxiety**: Without the pressure to be flawless, you can approach tasks with a sense of calm and confidence, reducing stress and anxiety.

Reflection Exercise

In your journal, take a few moments to answer these questions to deepen your understanding of perfectionism and cultivate a mindset of self-compassion:

- **How does perfectionism show up in my life, and how does it impact me?**
- **What would change if I allowed myself to pursue progress rather than perfection?**
- **How can I show myself kindness and compassion, even when I make mistakes?**

Affirmations for Letting Go of Perfectionism

Use these affirmations to support your journey of releasing perfectionism and embracing a balanced approach to growth:

- "I am enough as I am, and I am proud of my progress."
- "I celebrate my effort and embrace my imperfections with kindness."
- "I release the need for perfection, choosing growth and self-compassion instead."

Moving Forward with Balance and Self-Compassion

Letting go of perfectionism is an act of self-love and a step toward greater freedom and joy. By embracing imperfection, you're choosing a path that values growth, resilience, and authenticity. Remember, the journey is more important than the destination, and every step you take contributes to your growth, whether it's "perfect" or not.

As you continue this journey, practice treating yourself with patience and kindness. Celebrate the small victories, learn from challenges, and trust that you are enough, just as you are. Let today be a reminder that perfection is neither possible nor necessary for happiness. In releasing it, you're giving yourself the freedom to thrive, explore, and grow with a heart that is open, resilient, and full of grace.

Day 30: Reflecting on Your Transformation – A Vision for Your Future Self

Today marks the final day of this transformative journey. Over the past month, you've committed to growth, self-awareness, and positive change. You've learned to release limiting beliefs, embrace mindfulness, manage your time and energy, and cultivate inner peace. Now it's time to reflect on how far you've come and envision the person you are becoming—the future self that you are steadily stepping into.

Reflection is a powerful tool that allows you to celebrate progress, recognize strengths, and set intentions for the path ahead. By looking back on your journey, you can see the transformation that has taken place, both in small habits and in deeper shifts in mindset. Today, you'll reflect on this transformation and create a vision for your future self—a version of you that continues to grow, thrive, and embrace life with purpose and clarity.

Why Reflection and Vision Matter

Reflecting on your growth solidifies the progress you've made, allowing you to see your transformation as a foundation for future growth. When you look back with intention, you're able to recognize patterns, celebrate achievements, and carry forward valuable insights. Creating a vision for your future self gives direction to this growth, helping you set goals that align with your deepest values and aspirations.

Having a clear vision is like planting a seed for the life you wish to cultivate. By visualizing your future self, you're guiding your mind, heart, and actions toward becoming that person. This practice helps you stay grounded in your purpose, motivating you to continue on this path of self-discovery and positive change.

Reflecting on Your Transformation

Let's begin by looking back on the past 30 days. Use these prompts to help you reflect on your journey and recognize the transformation you've experienced:

1. **What are the Key Lessons I've Learned?**

- Think about the insights that stood out to you the most. Perhaps you discovered new ways to manage stress, cultivate gratitude, or let go of perfectionism. List the lessons that resonate deeply with you and have influenced how you view yourself and your life.
2. **How Have I Grown Emotionally, Mentally, or Spiritually?**
    - Reflect on any shifts you've noticed in your mindset, emotional resilience, or spiritual awareness. Do you feel more grounded, compassionate, or empowered? Consider the changes that have made a lasting impact on your well-being.
3. **What Habits or Practices Have Supported My Growth?**
    - Identify the habits and practices that you found most beneficial—whether it's journaling, mindfulness, breathing exercises, or setting boundaries. Recognizing these practices helps you see what's working and encourages you to continue with them.
4. **What Moments Am I Most Proud Of?**
    - Take a moment to celebrate your accomplishments, big and small. Maybe you showed kindness to yourself, faced a fear, or took a step toward a goal. Honor these moments as evidence of your commitment to growth and self-love.

Creating a Vision for Your Future Self

Now that you've reflected on your transformation, it's time to create a vision for your future self. This vision serves as a guiding light, motivating you to keep growing in ways that align with your values. Here's a step-by-step approach to crafting a powerful and inspiring vision for the person you are becoming:

1. **Imagine Your Ideal Life**:
    - Close your eyes and imagine yourself in the future, perhaps one year from now. Picture yourself living in alignment with your values, feeling fulfilled, balanced, and joyful. Visualize the life you're living, the people around you, and the impact you're making.

- o Allow yourself to dream big and embrace the possibilities. Notice how this vision makes you feel—perhaps peaceful, inspired, or confident.

2. **Describe Your Future Self**:
   - o Imagine the qualities, habits, and mindsets that define your future self. Are you more resilient, self-compassionate, mindful, or purposeful? Write down the characteristics that you aspire to embody.
   - o Be specific and positive, using present-tense language to affirm that these qualities are already within you, unfolding with each step forward.

3. **Identify Your Future Goals**:
   - o Based on your vision, set a few meaningful goals that will support you on this journey. These could be personal, professional, or spiritual goals—anything that aligns with the person you're becoming.
   - o Break down each goal into actionable steps, ensuring they are achievable and aligned with your values. Remember, these goals are not about perfection; they're about progress and intentional growth.

4. **List the Habits to Support Your Vision**:
   - o Think about the habits that will help you become your future self. Maybe it's continuing a gratitude practice, setting time for reflection, or creating a balanced routine. List the habits that align with your vision and keep you grounded in this journey.
   - o These habits serve as daily anchors, bringing you closer to your future self with each small action.

5. **Create a Personal Affirmation**:
   - o Write a personal affirmation that captures your vision and embodies the qualities of your future self. This affirmation will remind you of your purpose and keep you motivated on days when challenges arise.
   - o For example, "I am a strong, compassionate, and resilient person, growing each day in alignment with my true self." Repeat this affirmation daily to reinforce your commitment to your vision.

A Visualization Exercise for Your Future Self

Here's a simple guided visualization to help you connect with your future self:

1. **Find a Comfortable Position**: Close your eyes, take a few deep breaths, and let your body relax.
2. **Picture Your Future Self**: Imagine yourself in the future, living in alignment with your goals and values. See yourself embodying the qualities and strength you aspire to have.
3. **Feel the Emotions**: Notice the sense of peace, confidence, and fulfillment that radiates from your future self. Allow yourself to fully experience these emotions, knowing they are within reach.
4. **Express Gratitude**: Thank yourself for committing to this journey and for the progress you've made. Feel gratitude for both the present and the future you are creating.
5. **Hold the Vision**: Hold onto this vision for a few moments, breathing it in and feeling its energy. When you're ready, gently open your eyes, carrying this sense of purpose and peace with you.

Reflection Exercise

In your journal, answer these questions to help solidify your vision for your future self:

- **What qualities define my future self, and how can I begin embodying them today?**
- **What goals align with my vision, and what steps can I take to achieve them?**
- **How can I maintain the habits and practices that support my growth?**

Affirmations for Your Future Self

Use these affirmations to reinforce your vision and stay inspired on your journey:

- "I am growing into the person I am meant to be, with purpose and joy."
- "I trust in my journey, knowing each step brings me closer to my true self."
- "I am proud of my progress and committed to my future growth."

123

Moving Forward with Purpose and Vision

As you complete this 30-day journey, take a moment to honor the progress you've made and the person you're becoming. Transformation is not a destination; it's an ongoing process of learning, evolving, and embracing life with an open heart. With each step forward, you're creating a life that reflects your values, aspirations, and unique strengths.

Keep this vision of your future self as a source of inspiration, a reminder of the life you are intentionally building. Embrace each new day with the confidence that you are growing, thriving, and stepping into your purpose. Carry this sense of purpose and clarity with you, knowing that your journey is guided by your commitment to becoming the best version of yourself.

Thank you for choosing this journey of self-discovery and growth. The future you envision is within reach, one step at a time, and it's a beautiful journey you deserve to embrace. Keep moving forward with courage, compassion, and confidence, creating a life that feels authentic, meaningful, and filled with joy.

Conclusion

Congratulations on completing this 30-day journey of self-discovery, growth, and transformation. By committing to this path, you have not only explored new practices and mindsets but also developed a deeper connection to yourself and to the values that guide your life. Each day has been a step toward building resilience, cultivating inner peace, and aligning your actions with your true purpose. Now, as you reflect on all you've learned, know that the journey doesn't end here. It is only the beginning.

Throughout this journey, you've taken intentional steps to prioritize your well-being, strengthen your mindset, and embrace the qualities that help you thrive. You've discovered the power of mindfulness, learned to manage your energy, let go of perfectionism, and connected with your vision for the future. Each of these practices serves as a foundation for a life filled with purpose, clarity, and joy. By integrating these tools and insights into your everyday routine, you're creating a life that reflects the very best of who you are and who you aspire to be.

Carrying This Transformation Forward

Transformation is a continuous journey—a series of choices made each day. As you move forward, remember that growth happens gradually and that self-compassion is a vital part of this process. You'll have moments of progress, moments of challenge, and moments of learning. Embrace each with an open heart, knowing that every experience contributes to your personal evolution.

1. **Maintain Daily Practices**: Continue practicing the habits that have resonated most with you. Whether it's gratitude journaling, meditation, or setting boundaries, these practices anchor your intentions and help you stay aligned with your vision.

2. **Return to Your Vision**: Keep the vision of your future self as a guiding light. Use it as a source of inspiration when you feel uncertain or challenged. Remember that each step you take, no matter how small, brings you closer to the person you are becoming.

3. **Embrace Imperfection and Celebrate Progress**: Growth isn't about perfection; it's about consistent effort and learning. Celebrate each small victory, recognizing that every step forward is a testament to your commitment to personal growth.
4. **Nurture Self-Compassion**: There will be days when the journey feels challenging. During these times, remember to treat yourself with kindness and patience. Self-compassion is not only a gift you give yourself but also a powerful tool that sustains your resilience.

A Final Reflection

Take a moment now to reflect on how this journey has impacted you. Consider the ways you've grown, the insights you've gained, and the practices that have brought you peace. Allow yourself to feel gratitude for the courage and commitment you've shown. You have created meaningful change in your life—change that will continue to blossom as you move forward.

Thank You for Embracing Your Journey

Thank you for choosing this path and for investing in yourself. The courage, dedication, and openness you've shown are truly inspiring. As you continue on your journey, carry with you the knowledge that you have the tools and inner strength to face life's challenges with grace, resilience, and confidence.

May this journey be the beginning of a life filled with purpose, joy, and connection to your true self. You are empowered, capable, and worthy of all that you aspire to create. Step forward with courage, knowing that your journey is a gift—one that brings you closer to the person you were always meant to be.

Here's to your continued growth, joy, and fulfillment. The best is yet to come.

Milton Keynes UK
Ingram Content Group UK Ltd.
UKHW021526011224
451733UK00007B/194

9 781787 931046